STARTING A BUSINESS

A COMPLETE GUIDE TO STARTING & MANAGING YOUR OWN COMPANY

GORDON BROCKHOUSE

Deloitte & Touche

KEY PORTER BOOKS

Canadian Cataloguing in Publication Data
Brockhouse, Gordon
    Starting a business

ISBN 1-55013-148-6

1. Small business – Management.   2. New business enterprises – Management.   I. Title.

HD62.7.B76 1989   658'.022   C89-094081-9

Design: Denise Maxwell
Typesetting: Southam Business Information and Communications Group Inc.
Printed and bound in Canada

Key Porter Books Limited
70 The Esplanade
Toronto, Ontario
Canada M5E 1R2

90 91 92 93 5 4 3 2 1

Contents

ACKNOWLEDGMENTS

I would be remiss if I did not express my thanks to the scores of people whose assistance in this book was invaluable. I'm especially grateful to those entrepreneurs who shared their business experiences so openly: John Asa, Phillip Bliss, Edward Borins, Manfred Breunig, John Cameron, Norma Clement, Howard Cracower, Alistair Davidson, Graham Edwards, Gordon Hunter, Victor Kokeram, Tom Laanep, Dale McNichol, Don Michaels, Bill Mulock, Greg Pastic, Sybil Shore, Boyd Taylor and Larry Zepf.

And I'm equally grateful to the experts who were so generous with their time: Ian Cameron, Peter Cook, Terrence Dobbin, Steven Golick, Gerry LeJan, Russell Knight, Ray Kong, Derek Lackey, Jerry Levitan, Patrick McGrath, Virginia Miles, Joe Miller, Gar Pynn, Ron Rotenberg, Paul Schroeder, Robin Sheilds Teeger, Deborah Stern, Catherine Swift and David Wooley.

Thanks are also due to Randall Litchfield for his role in this book. Last, but by no means least, I must thank my dear wife, Yasmin, for her support and encouragement.

INTRODUCTION:
"If Only I Knew Then What I Know Now..."

In increasing numbers, Canadians are launching their own businesses. According to the Canadian Federation of Independent Business (CFIB), a Toronto-based organization that represents 80,000 small and medium businesses, 140,000 new businesses became operational during the year ending March 31, 1988. That's up 10 percent over the previous year. Indeed, the number of new Canadian businesses has increased every year since 1982.

This book is aimed at people who are thinking of joining the ranks of Canada's entrepreneurs. Perhaps you have an idea for a new product or service. Perhaps you have an opportunity to buy an existing business or a franchise. The purpose of this book is to outline some of the challenges you'll have to overcome in order to make your plan a commercial reality.

According to conventional wisdom, your chances of success aren't great. An old saw has it that four out of five new businesses fail within five years—or, to look at it from the other direction, only one in five succeeds. New data cast doubt on this "one-in-five" adage. At the Babson Entrepreneurship Conference in Calgary, in May 1988, Bruce Phillips of the U.S. Small Business Administration and Bruce Kirchhoff, professor of entrepreneurship at Babson College in Babson Park, Massachusetts, presented a paper on new-firm survival and growth. Based on information from the credit-reporting agency Dun & Bradstreet Corp., the authors conclude that 39.8 percent of new firms—almost two in five—formed between 1976 and 1978 survived at least six years.

Two-in-five odds are better than one-in-five. Instead of a long shot, survival of a new business is almost an even-money proposition, assuming Phillips's and Kirchhoff's analysis applies to Canada.

1

What separates the winners from losers? According to Catherine Swift, vice-president and chief economist for the CFIB, a major reason for business failures is underfinancing. Otherwise-viable young businesses are dragged down by onerous credit terms. "Financing can grease the wheels of a new business or throw a wet blanket on it," she comments. Another problem is marketing, or lack thereof. "Marketing is often treated as a frill," she notes. "It should be treated like finance, operations and other business activities. Often, new businesses don't do market research well, so they get surprises."

Joe Miller, vice-president and Ontario regional general manager for the Federal Business Development Bank (FBDB), doesn't think underfinancing is the main reason businesses fail. "Cash is like Aspirin," he comments. "It doesn't cure the disease, it just reduces the symptoms." Among the FBDB's programs is a consulting service for businesses with problems. "About 70 percent of the time, our clients identify symptoms, not problems. They may think they're undercapitalized, but in fact they're overstocked, or in a poor location, or they have shrinkage or control problems, or they've underestimated the competition.

"People usually start with enough money. The problem is they mismanage their businesses. We're not talking about people being stupid, we're talking about inexperience. People often go into business because they have one marketable skill. A plumber making $20 an hour may go into business because he sees his boss charging his time at $50 an hour. He doesn't know all the other things he has to do once he's running his own business. He has to hire right. He has to look after finance, accounting and administration. He has to be aware of local regulations. He has to tender for jobs, and to do selling and marketing. You can learn these things, but you have to be aware that you need to learn."

Many entrepreneurs would agree with Miller. While external factors play a part in many business failures, it's not uncommon to hear, "If only I knew then what I know now, this would never have happened."

In short, there are a lot of things entrepreneurs can do to improve their chances of success. That's what this book is about. Given the infinite variety of business opportunities in Canada, a book of this length can't pretend to answer every question about starting and managing a small business. But it can raise many of the questions business people should ask themselves. What does it take to manage a business successfully? Do I have what it takes? Is there a market for my product or service? How do I address that market? What kind of financing do I need? How do I obtain it? How do I choose a location? What should I look for in my employees? Where do I find them? How do I motivate them? What should I expect from my suppliers and professional advisers? How should I manage my money? How will my business be affected by federal, provincial and municipal laws?

In this book, you'll meet experts who can help answer these questions, entrepreneurs who've already faced these challenges. Some have been successful; others have not. All the entrepreneurs I interviewed for this book were frank about their mistakes. As one commented, "It's painful airing your dirty laundry in public." He spoke frankly because he hoped other business people could learn from his experience. I'm grateful to him and all the entrepreneurs who talked so openly about their business lives. You learn more from your failures than from your successes, a business truism has it. That may be so, but the tuition is very high. This book gives you a chance to learn from other entrepreneurs' mistakes.

Part I, "Starting the Business," deals with issues entrepreneurs have to address before opening their doors: researching the market, developing a business plan, obtaining financing, choosing a location. Part II, "Managing the Business," deals with day-to-day managerial issues: staffing, financial management, marketing. While these are all ongoing management challenges, obviously any business person must consider them before starting a new enterprise.

This book is intended as a guide through the numerous thorny paths to successful business entrepreneurship; however, each chapter can stand on its own. For example, if you're at the stage of choosing a location for your business, you can read that chapter before the preceding ones. In the end, the success of this book won't be measured so much by the answers it gives as by the questions it leads you to address. Similarly, the success of your business venture will be affected by your awareness of the need to deal with these questions.

PART I:
STARTING THE BUSINESS

1/THE RIGHT PEOPLE:
Skills and Talents You'll Need in Your Own Business

It took Manfred Breunig more than a decade to appreciate the complexity of running a business. After clinging to survival for 10 years, his Brampton, Ontario, stereo-equipment manufacturing company is now prospering in a market dominated by Japanese giants. There are many reasons for the turnaround, not least of which is an innovative new series of products. But a significant one is the team that is now operating the firm.

From 1966, when he founded Magnum Dynalab Ltd., to 1985, when he restructured the company, Breunig resisted taking on a partner. For its first 10 years, his company grew steadily; and by 1975 it was selling $850,000 worth of AM/FM receivers a year. Some were sold through independent retailers under the company's Magnum brand; others to corporate customers who put their own labels on the product. Then disaster struck. In late 1974, the distributor who handled Magnum-brand product simply stopped buying; and in late 1975, the firm's largest private-label customer informed him it planned to buy receivers from Japanese suppliers. The next year, Breunig's sales plunged to $200,000. For the next decade, he barely managed to survive, usually breaking even on annual revenues ranging from $200,000 to $250,000.

Then, in 1984, Breunig developed a unique upmarket tuner, sure to appeal to audiophiles. He realized he would need financial help to put the tuner into production, so he put the word out that he was looking for a partner. In the summer of 1985, Larry Zurowski injected $400,000 into the company in return for 51 percent ownership, and took over as president. He had recently sold his stake in a materials-handling company, and was looking for a company in the electronics business that had a unique product. Magnum

6

Dynalab qualified on both counts. Breunig became vice-president of design and manufacturing. He subsequently sold another 15 percent to Marv Southcott, the firm's director of marketing. "We wanted to lock him in," Breunig explains.

The triumvirate has worked well. Fiscal 1987-88 sales were $800,000, a 131 percent improvement over the previous year. The company is projecting $1.5 million for 1988-89. And the firm is profitable. Zurowski won't reveal how profitable, but says he aims for pre-tax profits of 22 percent.

Zurowski brought solid financial and administrative skills to the company. Southcott brought marketing skills, plus extensive contacts with audio dealers and audio-enthusiasts' magazines. Breunig's strengths are technical ones: product development and manufacturing, but he does not have the communication skills that distinguish a successful marketer. Further, during the firm's problem period, he was doing more than he could handle, and, as a result, was not always able to keep tabs on the company's financial situation. Even in the boom years of the mid-1970s, his firm wasn't making money once administrative costs were factored in. "Before I was trying to wear 15 hats at once," he comments. "Now I only have to wear 5." He says his partners' talents have been as important for the firm's revived fortunes as the cash they put into the company. He's happy with the new arrangements. "Owning 34 percent of a growing company beats owning 100 percent of a dead one," he comments.

Breunig's experience shows how vital it is for people entering business to take stock of their strengths and weaknesses. According to the Royal Bank of Canada, 90 percent of all business failures can be attributed to inexperienced or incompetent management. In other words, the entrepreneur's managerial skills are the number-one determinant of his or her chances for success.

TALENTS

PHYSICAL RESOURCES

As an owner/manager, you're going to need a fair bit of stamina. It's not uncommon for business owners to put in 60- and 80-hour weeks during the first couple of years. So think carefully about the time it will take to get your business going and about your own physical resources. Albert Friedman, an American businessman, has put together an "Entrepreneurial Test" for *Entrepreneur* magazine of Los Angeles, California. (The test is available from *Entrepreneur* magazine as part of a business manual and excerpts are printed here with its permission.) According to the test, if you're in good health, if you sleep fewer than eight hours a night, if you can work long stretches without getting fatigued, if you work well under pressure, if you work on weekends, if you sometimes get up early to work on special projects, if you get engrossed in tasks to the exclusion of all diversions, then you should have the stamina it takes to launch your own business.

FAMILY SUPPORT

Time devoted to your business will be time away from your family. That calls for understanding from your spouse and children. Are there special circumstances, such as illness in your family, that might affect the time you can allocate to your business? Are your family relationships sufficiently stable to sustain you through the inevitable ups and downs of starting a business? Do you have a circle of friends and associates from whom you can draw support?

DEALING WITH SETBACKS

What about your temperament? Can you handle the stresses that go along with being your own boss? Can you maintain self-control and balanced judgment in high-pressure situations? Will your ego be bruised by every setback, or can you learn from your mistakes and start over again? If you hate losing but can still see humour in your weaknesses, if you can evaluate your failures rationally, if you can restart a project after a serious setback, if you recover well when you're depressed, then you've passed the Entrepreneurial Test for handling the pressures and frustrations of running your own business.

DEALING WITH RISK

Starting your own business involves a calculated risk, giving up a benefits package and regular paycheque. Do you have confidence in your ability to make business risks pay off? In your own business, your future and your money, not someone else's, are on the line. If you believe that people shape their own fortunes, if you're generally optimistic about life, if you buy things on credit and aren't uncomfortable with being in a certain amount of debt, then chances are you can live with the risk of striking out on your own.

DISCIPLINE

Your business is going to depend on your drive to succeed. Are you disciplined? Do you have the "stick-to-it-iveness" to operate a business without a boss behind you? Planning is important too. Are you able to concentrate on important projects instead of being diverted by unimportant matters? If you have long-term financial goals, if you generally plan a course of action before jumping into a project, if you review progress during projects, if you see them through to the end, if at the end of a day you plan the next day's activity, then you probably have the discipline and perseverance to operate your own business.

RESPONSIBILITY

Except for major shareholders and CEOs, workers in the corporate world are responsible to someone else. In your own business, the buck stops with you. That means you have to set high standards for your own work—and meet them. If you finish projects and arrive at meetings on time, if you work to high standards, if you enjoy responsibility and new challenges, you have the self-reliance you'll need to be your own boss.

LEADERSHIP

A business owner is by definition a leader, to his or her employees and customers. Can you be fair but firm with employees? Can you set an example for how the business should be operated? Can you set consistent, fair policies? If you can get a point across without being obnoxious, if you're fairly immune to being sold a "bill of goods," if you enjoy working independently, if you try to conscript others to your point of view even when you're the only one in a group who holds it, if you're comfortable meeting new people, if you make friends easily, if you take the lead at conferences and business meetings, if people come to you for advice, if you've been involved in sales, then you have the leadership qualities you need in your own business.

COMMUNICATION SKILLS

What about your communications abilities? Especially if you are in a position where you interact with the public, you should evaluate your ability to state a position clearly, forcefully, tactfully and, where appropriate, with a touch of humour. If you enjoy speaking to audiences, if you can keep a conversation going, if you make it a point to maintain eye contact, if you match the level of your conversation to that of the other party, if you're a good listener, if you excel at written communications, then you're a good communicator and have a skill that is vital in operating your own business.

DECISIVENESS

Any business person is going to have to make important decisions that profoundly affect the business. How decisive a person are you? Can you make important decisions, or do you waffle? If you take the lead at conferences and business meetings, if you try to sell others on your ideas, if you like to be asked for advice, if you tend to dominate conversations, if you're active in politics or community work, particularly at senior levels, you probably have the decision-making ability you'll need as an owner/manager.

PROBLEM-SOLVING

Equally important is analytical ability. Business decisions often involve complex, and sometimes conflicting, considerations. The best course of action from a marketing point of view may be inappropriate from a financial or production standpoint. It's no good being decisive unless you base decisions on the appropriate facts. At the same time, operating your own business often requires that you make decisions fast, sometimes without all the pertinent information and often on the basis of hunches. Overanalysing a situation can cause you to miss opportunities. If you can handle several different demands at the same time, if you are comfortable without always knowing when or how money will come in, then you can live with the uncertainty that's part of running your own business.

GETTING HELP

To make good decisions you need good information. If you tend to ask people questions about their business lives, if you've ever sought the advice of a professional counsellor (for business or personal matters), if you seek the advice of experienced people, if you have a personal accountant or lawyer, if you've discussed your business plans with others, then you'll probably make appropriate use of others' ideas for making business decisions.

CREATIVITY

But entrepreneurs don't succeed by following the crowd. They're usually non-conformists, adept at spotting opportunities others have missed. Generally speaking, they're not joiners. If you regularly add a creative twist to others' ideas, if you can come up with different solutions for a particular problem, if you can alter plans quickly to adapt to changing circumstances, then you have some of the creative bent any entrepreneur needs.

Entrepreneurial traits are more common in immigrants than in natives, and in people whose immediate family members have operated their own businesses. Peter Cook, a Toronto businessman who lectures on entrepreneurship at Centennial College in Scarborough, Ontario, says three-quarters of the students in his courses have someone in their immediate family who's self-employed. Neither trend is surprising. Aptitudes that lead one to operating one's own business are either inherited or learned at home. Similarly, people with the drive to seek opportunities in a new country likely have the drive to pursue opportunities in their own businesses.

It's obvious that many entrepreneurial characteristics are contradictory. To succeed in your own business, you should have a creative streak that lets you see things others miss, but you should be able to see the value in others' ideas. You should have a drive to win and the ability to accept losses. While some of these traits are ingrained—inherited from parents or developed when young—others can be acquired. A robust constitution that lets you work long hours with little rest is probably inherited, but you can improve your stamina with good diet and regular exercise. Organizational and analytical abilities are partly ingrained, partly learned.

SKILLS

Just as important as character traits are managerial skills. Corporations are operated by specialists who know a lot about a narrow field. Independent businesses are run by generalists who can address the many facets of running a business: operations, finance, marketing, staffing. In your own business, you have to wear many hats. Before you launch your new enterprise, it's vital that you know what jobs you can do and what new skills you'll have to acquire.

HANDS-ON SKILLS

Quite likely, your greatest strength will be in the operational end of your business. If you're opening a store, you should know something about retail. If you're planning to manufacture widgets, you'll need to know about widget design. Such knowledge may be acquired from experience in the industry or from professional courses. However, specific expertise aside, you should consider all aspects of starting and running your business. You may have an idea for a specialty restaurant. Think about everything involved in running that kind of business: buying food, equipping and managing a kitchen, designing and equipping the serving room, hiring and training kitchen and serving help, avoiding spoilage and wastage, preventing shrinkage and so on. Similarly, retailers will want to consider not only the sales side of the business, but purchasing, advertising, store design, fixtures and fittings and inventory control. Besides knowledge of the product, a manufacturer needs to know about obtaining equipment and tools, designing a factory, sourcing materials, maintaining production schedules and controlling quality.

In addition to character traits, Albert Friedman's Entrepreneurial Test also tests business skills. If you subscribe to technical magazines related to your industry, if you read about matters outside your field of work, if you've taken courses to help you in your work in the last three years, if you know a lot about the business you're starting, if you regularly read business magazines and news magazines, if you've ever supervised people, you should have the kind of hands-on skills, or at least an understanding of how to acquire them, to make your business run smoothly, and successfully.

CONTACTS
Experience in your industry is important for another reason: contacts you've developed over the years may become customers for your new enterprise. And experience will tell you which suppliers are reliable, and which ones aren't; which ones have the best terms and which ones promote most aggressively.

MARKETING
Important as the operational end is, it's only one part of running a business. To succeed, you have to get customers to buy your product or service. That often involves far more than selling. As we'll see in later chapters, you have to determine just who your customers are, and whether they want what you're offering. It's a two-way street: you have to identify their needs, and tailor your product or service to those needs. You have to analyse their buying habits. You have to evaluate the size of the market, and your potential share. You have to

pinpoint competitors, and the best ways of enticing their customers. You have to calculate the price the market is willing to pay for your product, and what it will cost to produce it. In addition to sales skills, you have to be able to determine the information you need to market effectively, find out where to get it, then act on it.

FINANCE

It also takes financial expertise to run a business. In the start-up phase, you have to determine the financial needs of the venture—how much money it will take to get the business on its feet. You have to know what it will cost to equip your business, and how much working capital you'll need. You have to forecast sales, expenses, and profits and losses. You have to identify sources of funding: your own investment dollars, trade credit from suppliers, bank loans, equipment leases, government funding, money from other investors. Then you have to put the package together. That will often involve producing documents that address the concerns of potential lenders and investors. These documents include a business plan, information on the outlook of your industry, a statement of personal net worth and a personal credit record.

That's just the beginning. Expertise will be needed for the day-to-day financial management of your business: cashflow, collections, budgeting and so on. To manage effectively, you need to know your business's financial situation. Without good information, you leave yourself open to fraud or serious losses in the event of a catastrophe, such as a fire. You may spend money on improvements when you can't afford to. You may make serious mistakes in pricing, resulting in losses when you think you're making a profit. Sales may be declining, or expenses may be increasing, eroding your profit. You can't keep this information in your head. You need good records, and the ability to interpret them.

According to the *Entrepreneur* magazine's test, if you believe in the free-enterprise system, if you know basic bookkeeping principles, if you understand terms like "aged accounts receivable," if you know how to read a financial statement, you should have the "numbers sense" to operate your own business. It takes "money sense" to run a business too. If you've never been in debt over your head, if you carry life insurance, if you have a will, if you take money seriously, you should have the respect for money an independent business person needs.

BEING THE BOSS

Unless you're the only person who will work in the company, you'll need some personnel skills. First of all, you'll have to define the skills you need in your employees. You'll have to attract applicants, then evaluate them. Once you've hired employees, you'll have to train them. You'll have to assign them work, then supervise and motivate them. You'll have to evaluate their performance periodically, rewarding or disciplining them when appropriate. You'll have to maintain personnel records. To attract and keep capable people, you'll have to offer competitive salaries and benefits, and provide a work atmosphere conducive to productive labour. You'll have to set policies for breaks, vacations and so on. You may have to deal with a union. Hiring employees exposes you to all kinds of legal obligations, including, withholding taxes, making contributions to Unemployment Insurance and the Canada Pension Plan, maintaining safe working conditions and following prescribed labour practices.

RUNNING THE SHIP

Closely related to staffing skills is the ability to manage; it is crucial that staff are directed to do the work management deems necessary to advance the company's interests. Certainly, delegating is one important aspect of management; and you should evaluate your skills in this area. Other important skills are planning—determining the business's goals and the best ways of achieving them—problem-solving and decision-making.

That's a formidable array of talents and skills. Do you really need all these to succeed in your own business? Entrepreneurship lecturer Peter Cook says no. "You need three things: financial and accounting skills so you can control your business, marketing flare and administrative skills. You can always hire a programmer or a plant supervisor. The guy you can't replace is the guy who has these three things." Cook says what separates the entrepreneurial from the conventional mind is intuition: the ability to perceive an opportunity, then act on it without overanalysing it. "An entrepreneur can relate to things someone with a more pragmatic mind might miss."

GETTING THE RIGHT MIX

It's not unlikely that you're short on some of the skills and traits noted above. And it may be that in your business, some of them aren't critical. What is important is that you take an inventory of your own strengths and weaknesses, and the skills and traits needed to operate your business successfully. The next logical question is, "How do I acquire the ones I'm missing?"

ACQUIRING SKILLS

There are lots of possibilities. First of all, you can learn on your own. You can read, or take courses. It is hoped that this book will help you in your business ventures; and there will be several more in this series dealing with specific aspects of small-business management. Many universities and community colleges offer business-management courses, some specifically on small business. Municipalities often present no-charge half-day seminars on small-business management. Most provincial and some municipal governments operate small-business self-help centres to assist entrepreneurs to shore up their management skills. Accounting and consulting firms offer courses and seminars on a variety of business-related topics.

If you're short on operational skills, you may find courses offered at colleges helpful. In addition to trades programs, retail merchandising, food and beverage, hotel management and a host of other courses are available. Whether you're looking for general management or industry-specific courses, your public library is a good place to start. It should have calendars that list courses available at Canadian colleges and universities, many of them offered part time, during the evening. The reference librarian will be able to help you find what you want.

Trade associations are a worthwhile source of industry-specific information. In addition to printed material, many offer useful courses, often at their annual conventions. Suppliers are also a valuable source of information. In addition to product-specific training, many suppliers will provide training on their industry and general business methods. After all, it's in a supplier's interest to see its clients succeed.

It's a lot easier to acquire a skill before you start your business than after. Once you've opened your doors, you'll probably be so occupied with day-to-day operations you won't have time for catch up learning.

It's one thing to learn a skill; it's another to develop a character trait (or, at least, to compensate for a weakness). Skills are learned; character traits are deeply ingrained. But as the experience of thousands shows, weaknesses can be overcome. You *can* learn to communicate, or to analyse information, or to make decisions more effectively. Identifying a weakness is the first step to overcoming it.

HIRING SKILLS

Rarely will a single individual be ideally equipped to handle all the aspects of a given business. One obvious alternative is to hire the skills you need. If you're a good marketer but a poor administrator, hire a controller. If you possess excellent analytical skills but limited communications skills, hire a marketing manager.

Often a business will need specific skills for just a limited time. If you're computerizing your accounting system, you'll need someone who can help you choose (or develop) the right software for your business, help with the transition from manual to computerized record-keeping and train your staff. Often businesses have to seek outside expertise for these tasks. Since these specific skills are required for only a few weeks or months, it doesn't really make sense to hire someone with them on a permanent basis. That's when it makes sense to retain a consultant.

Joe Miller, vice-president and Ontario regional general manager for the Federal Business Development Bank, says some businesses recruit people in their communities to act as an informal board of directors. The business owners will meet with the "board" over breakfast once or twice a month to pick their brains. "If they take an interest in your operation," he adds, "they can be a source of business as well."

FINDING A SKILLED PARTNER

Another alternative to wearing all the hats yourself is to bring in a partner. This approach has several advantages. One, and not the least of them, is that a partner could bring capital into the business. Also, making a talented person a partner ties him or her to your enterprise, and limits the possibility that that valuable person will work for a competitor. And someone who owns a piece of the

business will work harder than someone who is simply employed
by it.

However, people are often loath to take on a partner because it
inevitably entails sacrificing some control of the business. That's
understandable. Horror stories about bad partnerships are almost as
common as those about bad marriages. But in addition to capital, a
partner can bring vital skills to a business, as Magnum Dynalab's
history illustrates.

ORGANIZING THE COMPANY

You'll have to devote careful thought to how your business is
organized, and the agreements that cover its organization. First, you
have to determine whether to incorporate, or run the business as a
sole proprietorship (if you're the sole owner) or a partnership. When
a corporation is formed, shares are issued to the owners. The
proportion of total shares issued to each reflects the proportion of
the company each partner owns.

The major advantage of incorporation is, of course, limited
liability. With a corporation, the company and its shareholders are
legally separate. Should the business fail, only its assets can be seized
by creditors, that is, the owners' personal assets are exempt. (In the
real world that's not strictly true, since most startups have to offer
personal guarantees to obtain financing.) With a proprietorship or
partnership, the company and its owner(s) are fully responsible for
all liabilities incurred by the business. If the business fails, business
and personal assets can be seized to cover its debts. If you do not
incorporate, you should take steps to minimize the risk of unlimited
liability. This may be accomplished by arranging liability insurance,
and, where possible, having your spouse hold family assets.

To Incorporate . . .
There are other issues to be considered when deciding whether or not
to incorporate. Incorporation offers significant income-splitting and
tax-deferral possibilities. You can arrange your fiscal year so that
you delay the onset of tax liability. You can minimize tax by the
appropriate division of income between the business (profits) and its
owners (dividends and salaries). Since partnerships and proprietor-
ships are not legally distinct from the owners, owners pay personal
income tax on business profits. It's easier to change ownership with a

corporation; shares are simply exchanged. Because the liability of investors is limited, it can be easier to raise capital. (In most cases, this is a minor consideration, since most small businesses depend on debt rather than equity financing.)

... OR NOT TO INCORPORATE

But there are disadvantages to incorporating. For one thing, setting up a corporation is a complex and expensive legal procedure. With a proprietorship or partnership, you just register your business name with the appropriate agency for a small fee. Incorporating also entails higher ongoing professional fees. In a corporation, separate tax returns have to be filed for the company and its owners. Corporations face considerable record-keeping requirements and government regulations. Finally, operating losses of the business can't be used to reduce its owners' personal taxes.

In general, it's better to operate as a partnership or proprietorship if you expect the business to generate losses that can be used to reduce your personal taxes and if you won't benefit from the tax-deferral and income-splitting opportunities of a corporation. But if your business requires major startup and ongoing financing, if your staffing requirements are sizable or if you expect to generate large profits, it's better to incorporate. Whichever route you take, get professional advice from your lawyer and accountant.

Unless you're operating as a sole proprietorship, you'll also need professional help drafting a partnership or shareholder's agreement. In addition to detailing relative ownership of the company, such an agreement should list responsibilities. And since relationships between partners don't always proceed smoothly, it should contain a means for settling disputes and, if necessary, arranging buyouts.

Buyouts don't always arise from disputes. The death or disability of a partner can necessitate a buyout. Many businesses carry insurance on the owners' lives so that, if one owner dies, the others can use the proceeds to buy the deceased's share from his or her estate or spouse. Insurance is available to finance buyouts in the event of a partner's becoming disabled, but it is expensive.

Many partnership agreements contain a "shotgun clause" as their ultimate dispute-settling mechanism. Under this kind of agreement, one partner can offer to buy the other (or others) out, with the understanding that the other can buy him or her out for the same per-share price. Shotgun clauses offer disputing partners a way out of an impasse that might have no other solution. And in theory, they ensure fairness. If one partner offers the other an unacceptably low price, he or she could be setting the selling-price of his or her own shares. Also common are competition clauses, which bar the selling partner from competing with his or her old firm for a specified period.

Shotgun clauses are open to abuse, says Toronto businessman Gordon Hunter. President of The Hunter Group, which produces trade and consumer shows for the food, sporting-goods and computer industries, Hunter has been involved in partnerships that work well, and one that didn't. He says he's seen many instances of people waiting until a partner is in a difficult financial situation, then offering a low-ball price for his or her shares, knowing that there's no way the partner can raise the money for a counteroffer. "It happens all the time. People wait till their partner is in a negative situation, then spring the shotgun." Shotgun clauses are supposed to protect partners from unreasonable buyout attempts. But Hunter says third-party evaluations from independent parties such as accounting firms achieve the same end.

SOME PARTNERSHIPS WORK ...

Hunter recalls being asked about partnerships by a businessman he knew casually. A mutual friend had suggested to Ted Simon that he speak to Hunter about the art business he was planning. Simon wanted to sell limited-edition reproductions of works by top international artists that sold as originals for $5,000 to $50,000. The plan was "to make unaffordable art affordable." He was contemplating a partnership to raise the capital he needed. The friend thought Simon might profit by learning about Hunter's experience with a partnership that didn't work out.

Avoid a purely financial partnership, Hunter advised him. "My experience is that people come to resent financial partners," he comments. "At first, they respect the money the partner has provided. But later, they see themselves doing all the work and sharing the rewards with someone who doesn't work." Instead, one should seek a partner with a working knowledge of the industry who can make a contribution in the business.

He advised Simon to seek a partner with deep pockets, instead of just enough money to cover the initial investment. Startup businesses almost always underestimate what it will cost to get up and running,

Hunter notes. Simon would probably have to go to the well often before his business got off the ground.

As it turned out, he did; and it was Hunter who gave him the backing. Simon had been considering a financial partnership. Hunter described the kind of partner he should seek, and added, "Someone like me."

"Is that an offer?" Simon asked. "I hadn't thought about it," replied Hunter. "Would you be interested in seeing my business plan?" Hunter was. An art collector himself, he was attracted by the opportunity to create a new type of business. At that time, he was involved in magazine publishing, so knew the printing problems that Simon Art would face. His administrative and marketing skills complemented Simon's artistic judgment, contacts with galleries and artists and knowledge of printing. "There are clearcut areas where we're each strong," Hunter comments.

It took a few months to arrange the partnership, during which time they ironed out kinks in Simon's business plan. As is true in most startups, Simon hadn't considered many of the hidden costs of launching a new venture. "You have to buy everything, from paperclips up," Hunter notes.

Simon took Hunter's advice. In 1981, he sold Hunter a stake in Simon Art Ltd. that was slightly less than 50 percent. Hunter was involved in the business from day one, in a consultative role at first. Every month, they'd pore over the financial statements together. As the business grew, so did Hunter's role; by 1989 it was taking up more than half his time.

And as Hunter had predicted, Simon returned several times for additional financing. Finally, in 1985, Hunter had to draw the line. Instead of pouring more money into the firm, Hunter told Simon they had to find another way to make the business work, or let it fail. They made it work.

Hunter says he's "long since" recovered his total investment in Simon Art. He won't reveal sales or profits, but says sales doubled every year from 1985 to 1989. The partnership obviously has worked well. But as already noted, Hunter has also had bad experiences with partnerships.

... OTHERS DON'T

In 1985, Hunter bought out a long-standing partner in his publishing-tradeshow business after a dispute about the partner's contribution to the company. Following the expiry of a non-competition clause, the former partner launched a tradeshow in direct competition with one of Hunter's. "There are always repercussions when a partnership breaks up," Hunter comments. "It's best to be prepared for them."

Because the shareholders' agreement had been carefully drafted, the breakup was far less complex than it might have been. Hunter's partner had 25 percent of the firm. At the time the partnership was arranged, Hunter had specified that he'd retain control of the company. He set it up according to the advice he later gave Simon. The partner could sell his share only to Hunter. A fair price would be determined by a mutually satisfactory third party. Hunter could sell the company if he wanted, but he'd have to give his partner first right of refusal. Thus, when relations between the two reached the breaking-point, the resolution was relatively simple.

When two people marry, they expect to stay together. It's the same with business partners. In an ideal world, divorce laws and buyout clauses would never be invoked. The secret to making a partnership work is the same as making a marriage work, Hunter says. "Like marriage, the biggest problem that can affect a partnership is poor communication. If something is bothering you, you have to address it immediately. If you don't nip it in the bud, it will poison the relationship."

Owners affect their businesses' fortunes more than any other factor. It takes just the right mix of talents and skills for a business to succeed. Sometimes, one person has all the ingredients for the venture's success; sometimes it takes the talents of several people. Regardless of the structure, the owners have to work effectively, and they have to work together.

2/"Good Idea, Eh?":
Evaluating Your Business Opportunity

For Victor and Soma Kokeram, buying the NS Restaurant in Montreal seemed like the perfect opportunity. Soma's brother Emrith Kalliecharan had been operating a bustling restaurant for eight years, serving roti and other Caribbean dishes to Montreal's West Indian community. The Kokerams thought they could repeat Emrith's success in a different neighbourhood.

The couple had worked in family businesses in their native Trinidad: Soma in her family's department store, Victor in his family's restaurant. Between the two of them, they had the experience to manage their own business. And the operation looked good. The owner was retiring after running the restaurant for 20 years. People in the neighbourhood spoke favourably of it. Victor showed the firm's books to several people—his accountant, Kalliecharan and a friend who operated a small restaurant chain. Given the daily sales of $300 to $400 shown in the books, all agreed the business was well worth the $35,000 asking price. The Kokerams got a loan to finance the purchase, and took possession in December 1985. The price covered the lease, equipment and goodwill.

They had plans to increase sales. To the regular greasy-spoon menu they would add the Caribbean dishes that were doing so well in Emrith's restaurant, less than a five-minute drive away from theirs.

Things never worked out. The Caribbean fare didn't catch on with the Kokerams' clientele. Sales were one-third those shown on the previous owner's books. Victor acknowledges that some of the restaurant's regulars stopped coming: but he also wonders whether the books gave an accurate picture of the business. Receipts covered such expenses as food, rent, utilities and staff, but the Kokerams had to dip into their savings to make payments on the loan. Victor estimates that during the three years they operated the restaurant, they lost $25,000. When Soma became ill in mid-1988, they had to sell. They got only $17,000.

Meanwhile, Kalliecharan's business is still thriving. Non-Caribbeans also flock there to enjoy West Indian dishes. As it turned out, more West Indians lived near Emrith's restaurant than near the Kokerams'. The short distance that separates the two restaurants was critical. So was Emrith's restaurant's reputation. The Kokerams never managed to build up a following with fans of Caribbean food. The fact that his restaurant had no tables and chairs, only a counter, also hurt him, Victor says. But adding them would have involved a major renovation.

"I expected the restaurant to catch on by itself," he reflects. "If I were doing it again, I'd do a lot more research. I'd stake the place out for a month to find out what sales really were. And I'd survey the clientele to find out what they really want."

His lament is a common one. Most entrepreneurs whose ventures don't work out say they should have done more research. It's a task undertaken by too few new businesses, says Catherine Swift, chief economist for the Canadian Federation of Independent Business (CFIB). "Often, new businesses don't do market research well, so they get surprises. There may be no demand for their product, or the market may be smaller than anticipated. The market may be more competitive than first thought, or it may not be open to a new supplier. Demand thought to be elastic may be fixed."

Whether you're buying a new business, entering a franchise system or launching a new enterprise, you should evaluate the business opportunity before jumping in. In fact, basic research is an essential prerequisite for obtaining financing. You have to determine whether there's a market for your product; and how you can fine-tune your product to maximize the market. You have to determine what price the market's willing to pay for your product. You have to determine whether you can produce it profitably at that price. In short, you have to determine whether the idea behind your venture is a sound one.

In all these deliberations, you have to look at the long-term picture. Are local economic conditions changing in a way that could affect your venture? If a large employer is about to close shop, retail sales in the area would decrease. Is the business open to competition?

A local restaurant might get blown away if a franchised chain opens across the street. Could new technology affect the market for your product?

RESEARCHING AN EXISTING BUSINESS

Buying an existing business has several advantages over starting from scratch: existing customers, established location, relationships with suppliers, trained employees. If the operation is well managed, it has probably adjusted well to local conditions. That means less fine-tuning will be needed. But as the Kokerams' experience confirms, buying an existing business isn't a sure-fire route to success.

You can find out about businesses for sale in newspapers, business magazines and trade magazines. Bankers, accountants and lawyers often know of businesses for sale. If you're targeting a specific industry, talk to suppliers and customers in that field.

DOING YOUR HOMEWORK

A purchase opportunity is considerably easier to evaluate than is a new business opportunity. The previous owner's history can help you form your own projections. Still, as the Kokerams discovered, it's not enough to accept the seller's claims about a business. After all, to make the sale, a certain amount of lily-gilding will take place. You have to do some independent research to confirm the seller's claims.

You should first determine the vendor's reasons for selling. Is the owner retiring, or is the business not doing well? Review the operation. Just hanging around the business for a few days will tell you if it's as healthy as the owner claims. Talk to suppliers, customers, employees, the owner's banker and lawyer to get a feel for the company. Suppliers can tell you whether the owner pays bills on time, or has consistent cashflow problems. Interviewing staff can show you weaknesses in the business, and help you decide which employees to keep. Talking with customers will tell you how much goodwill the business enjoys, and how much is associated with the owner. Remember to assess the business's future prospects as well as its current situation. If you're buying a store or restaurant, find out if the neighbourhood is improving, stable or declining.

If the business has had problems (for example, if you're buying the assets of a bankrupt company), you have to have a plan to turn the operation around. Presumably, there was some flaw in the business that caused its problems. For the purchase to make sense, you have to identify the flaw, and deal with it.

REVIEW THE RECORDS

You should review the seller's financial statements for the past five years, and assess their reliability. Audited statements aren't a 100 percent guarantee of accuracy, but they offer the highest degree of reliability an accountant can offer. If statements have been audited, it means an accountant has gone over all the business's records to try to confirm their accuracy. If the statements have been reviewed rather than audited, the accountant has assessed the plausibility of the firm's statements to ensure they make sense in the circumstances and that they conform to generally accepted accounting principles. The third tier is a "notice to reader." This offers little assurance of reliability. The accountant is relying on the company's records to produce financial statements. The information has not been audited or reviewed as to its accuracy or completeness.

JUST WHAT ARE YOU BUYING?

It's also vital to know what it is you're buying. Are you buying all assets, including inventory and receivables? Can receivables be collected? Is inventory and equipment current, damaged or obsolete? Are you assuming existing debts? All these issues influence the effective purchase price of the business. And the purchase price, of course, affects the profitability of the business. As happened with the Kokerams, paying off an inflated purchase price can make it impossible to make a profit on the business. Your accountant should review the business's records to confirm the accuracy of claims for sales, inventory and accounts receivable.

As with a house purchase, the seller's price isn't necessarily the price you'll pay for the business. The seller may overvalue the business because of an emotional attachment. As with real estate, businesses are sometimes available from "motivated sellers," those who, for some reason, badly want to sell. That, of course, affects the selling price. Negotiating a price isn't unlike negotiating a house price. You'll do a lot better if you've done your research, and decided ahead of time the top price you're willing to pay.

MAKING THE DEAL

Prices for an existing business can be calculated several different ways. The "book value" of a business is the difference between the recorded value of assets, such as equipment, inventory and accounts receivable, and liabilities, such as trade debt and bank loans. However, book value isn't always a reliable indicator of potential profits. To use an absurd example, a buggy-whip manufacturer might have a high book value, but its future profitability is nil.

"Replacement value" shows the cost of acquiring comparable business assets at today's value, less liabilities. Since a new business will have new equipment, replacement value isn't necessarily a reliable indicator of the firm's value. Similarly, an existing business will have intangible assets such as goodwill, which are difficult to put a dollar value on.

Alternatively, you can base value on the business's earnings. Decide how many years you're willing to wait to recover your investment. Multiply that by the firm's average earnings and you get a value based on capitalized earnings. For a more rigorous way of assessing a business's value, you can apply the discounted cash flow method described in Chapter 11.

TERMS

You may be able to spread payments out over time. Besides reducing your up-front costs, that may reduce the seller's tax exposure. You may be able to reduce your risk by basing the price on future earnings. If there's a danger the seller may re-enter business in competition with you, put a non-competition clause in the agreement of sale. This clause will cover a fixed period, possibly five years, and/or a specified geographic region. If you need the seller's skills, consider a managed buyout. Essentially, that means the seller stays on as an employee while you learn the business.

When negotiating for the business, bear in mind its earnings potential under *your* management. Are you going to make changes to enhance the firm's earning potential? If the purchase is based on current earnings, you might end up with a bargain. Always keep in mind your top price, and be willing to walk away from the deal if it isn't right. Like a house purchase, you'll be living with the consequences long after you've signed the agreement. Get an opinion on the purchase from your accountant, and have your lawyer look at the purchase agreement.

RESEARCHING A FRANCHISE

On the face of it, buying a franchise is one of the safest ways to get into business for yourself. For one thing, you get a complete turn-key operation. You're buying into a successful business concept developed by the franchisor, rather than taking a risk on an unproven concept. If you're buying a mature franchise, you get an established name, instead of having to build your own reputation. Because buying a franchise from an established company is less risky than starting your own business, it's easier to get financing. It's usually easier to get prime retail locations. Major malls deal mainly with chain stores. Rarely will they lease to independents or startups.

Your success as a franchisee will depend on how well you use the resources provided by the franchisor. But it will also depend on the quality of those resources. There are risks in buying a franchise, as there are in entering any business.

Some people aren't suited to running a franchise. Sometimes, franchisees are saddled with poor locations. Sometimes, franchisors don't live up to their end of the bargain. Sometimes, relations between franchisor and franchisee are marred by personality clashes. And sometimes, franchisors go out of business, taking the franchisees' money with them. That's why it's so important to research the franchise opportunity before committing to it.

Horror Stories
Consider Tom Laanep's experience. A professional engineer, he bought a franchise from Vancouver-based TAB Publishing, after he became a victim of employer downsizing. The company was offering franchises in *Magascene*, a monthly consumer electronics magazine distributed to readers free of charge through audio-video retailers. While the publication's editorial content was the same across the country, regional editions were published to accommodate local dealer advertising. Only the inside covers were reserved for national advertisers. Each franchisee was granted a territory and received 10,000 copies of the edition for his or her region. It was up to franchisees to sell local ads and distribute the magazines. They billed local advertisers and kept the proceeds.

After a trip to Vancouver where he met management and discussed the operation, Laanep decided to buy a franchise for Brampton and Mississauga, Ontario. In late December 1986, he paid an upfront franchise fee of $20,000, and agreed to pay $7,500 a month for his magazines plus a 9 percent royalty on his billings.

Things never worked for him. The first issue Laanep tried to sell was April 1987. Because they had never seen the magazine, local retailers balked at buying ads. "It was a tough sell," he recalls. "It's like anything new. No one wanted to be the first to jump in." The May issue was late, which threw advertisers' promotional plans off. The magazine didn't publish at all in June or July. The August issue was an important one, as it functioned as the guide for a major Toronto audio-video equipment show. It was successful, but Laanep says TAB's management didn't follow up with national advertisers. They failed to publish in September, but did get the October issue out. It was the last one. The public company was experiencing financial difficulties, and was trying to raise money on the Vancouver Stock Exchange, or alternatively, to sell the publishing venture. After the October stock market crash, the company was insolvent.

The timing was unfortunate. By the fall, Laanep was selling $5,000 to $6,000 a month in local advertising—a far cry from the $20,000 a sold-out issue would bring, but up considerably from April and May. He says he averaged $2,500 an issue over the four issues he received. With the franchisor's insolvency, Laanep was out $20,000. A lawyer advised him against suing, since his agreement was with the insolvent division, not with the parent company. Laanep was also out the time he spent developing his business. He notes that the franchisor waived the $7,500 fee and 9 percent royalty for the lean April and May issues, and charged only $2,500 for August.

MANAGEMENT QUALITY

Laanep blames the failure squarely on TAB's management. "There were no controls. There was no one in charge of the purse strings." But he still has faith in the concept behind the franchise. "If they could have got out one more issue, I think it could have done well. I think the basic idea was good, but they needed better management."

Franchisees have little recourse if a franchisor goes out of business. Sometimes companies start franchising to alleviate a tight cashflow position or because they have been unable to secure financing for expansion. That's why it's so important to research the quality of management and financial stability before committing. Franchisees should determine the length of time the franchisor has been operating, and the number of locations. If possible, they should get credit references.

They should talk to industry associations about the franchisor, and especially to other franchisees to determine how well the franchisor has lived up to his or her promises. They should determine the number of people giving support to franchisees, performing such services as sourcing new product and better suppliers, and co-ordinating P.R. and advertising. Training is also important. A good franchisor offers franchisees training in its products and its procedures, as well as in general business matters such as financial management, advertising, and hiring and training staff.

Laanep says he researched management quality when he visited Vancouver in December 1986. "I questioned them about everything I could think of: their background, their company's financial situation, the potential of the franchise and why they thought it represented a new market niche. They did a good selling job. The operation looked good from a cursory view, but I couldn't get answers about the nuts and bolts of the company." In retrospect, Laanep says he should have delved more deeply into the background of TAB's principals. "The biggest problem was dealing at a distance. If I had been local, I could have dug into the background of the people better. As it was, it was hard to get personal information or references."

Risk of franchisor failure is greater with new than with established franchises. Also with a new franchise, the franchisor's name isn't as well recognized. But there can be benefits. With a new franchise, you may have better choice of locations, and the terms may be better. In other words, the risks involved in a new franchise are greater, but the rewards may be as well.

GETTING SUPPLIES

At the very least, franchisees can protect themselves by ironing out in advance what happens if the franchisor experiences financial problems. If the franchisor is the sole supplier, you should be permitted to obtain supplies elsewhere if it can't supply.

If the franchisor is acting as supplier, potential franchisees should also evaluate pricing. Prices should not exceed what you'd pay on the open market, and should even be less. Because a franchisor has more buying power than a single franchisee, better prices may be negotiated through discounts and volume rebates. But franchisees shouldn't expect to get product at the franchisor's cost. Franchisees should also determine the return policy for defective goods, and whether goods can be transferred between locations.

COSTS

Besides profit on product, franchisors receive upfront franchise fees and monthly royalties, usually a percentage of gross sales, plus an advertising allowance, and also a percentage of gross. The franchise fee doesn't buy a permanent arrangement, but rather one limited in time, sometimes to 10 years, sometimes for the life of the lease of the franchise location. Often there is provision for a one-term renewal for a fee. Many franchisees feel this arrangement is unfair. They compare it to buying a job. Actually, what they're buying is a licence. The length of the agreement should give you time to pay your loans and make some money.

Similarly, many franchisees object to royalties and advertising charges, often justifiably. They may be paying for an advertising program that achieves little penetration in their market areas. Many franchisors can't afford national advertising programs. Some will allow franchisees to apply part of their allowance to local advertising.

Some franchisees believe that it's a conflict of interest for a franchisor to operate company stores. However, company stores give the franchisor a place to train new franchisees and to try new products. They keep the franchisor in direct contact with consumers. Company stores become a problem, however, if the franchisor cherry-picks the best locations, and gives the dregs to franchisees.

LOCATION

So, it's important to research the individual location, as well as the franchise operation. Check the franchisor's research about the location. If it's the first location in a new area, determine the franchise's chances of success in that area. Many of the methods outlined below for evaluating a new business opportunity can be used for evaluating a franchise location.

Above all, no one should ever buy a franchise conditionally, without a designated location. If you must enter a franchise agreement before you have a site, at the very least make sure there's an escape clause that lets you out of the agreement if you can't agree on a location.

DISPUTES

Disputes about location can occur after the agreement is signed. Bill and Judy bought a franchise in a gourmet coffee and tea chain after moving to Toronto from Montreal in 1981. (Because the couple and other former franchisees are involved in legal action with the franchisor, we're not using their real names.) They paid $155,000 for a five-year franchise for a kiosk in a major suburban mall; renewal for a second five-year term was at the franchisor's option. Two years later, they paid $90,000 for a second franchise: a storefront location in an upscale Toronto neighbourhood. They ran into problems when the storefront building was sold a year and a half later. The new landlord renewed the lease till the end of the year. Meanwhile the franchisor kept promising a new location, but, when the lease expired, didn't have one. He offered only to put the franchise "in storage" till a new location could be found.

Rather than waiting indefinitely for a new location, Bill and Judy talked to their lawyer. He advised them to take down the franchise sign and continue operation. That's what they did, after negotiating a 10-year lease from the new landlord. They say they never received any explanation from the franchisor about the failure to renew the lease. "Maybe they didn't pursue it," Bill speculates. A couple of months later, the franchisor complained that the couple were in default of royalty fees even though they were no longer operating under the franchise umbrella. The couple maintained that, by not renewing the lease or finding a location, the franchisor was in breach of its agreement. But they didn't take legal action, because the franchise agreement for the mall location was coming up for renewal.

Two weeks before that agreement expired, they were told to get out. No reason for the refusal to renew was given, only that it was "a corporate decision." The contract had no provision for automatic renewal. They say that when they signed the contract, they were given oral assurances that renewal would not be a problem. But the partner who made that promise subsequently left the company. The used fixtures, for which they had paid $40,000, reverted to the franchisor when it claimed it had only leased them to Bill and Judy. At that point, they decided to sue for breach of contract.

Besides the franchisor's failure to obtain a new storefront location and refusal to renew the agreement for the mall location, they claim that the franchisor never delivered anything for the 2 percent advertising fee. A Calgary franchisee, who saw two franchises put on hold after the franchisor failed to renew leases, and was in danger of losing a third, desperately tried to find a location on her own. When she did, she was told she could have the new location for a $190,000 franchise fee, even though two of her franchises were in storage. She's one of 14 other former franchisees suing the company.

Meanwhile, Bill and Judy have renamed and redecorated their store. They've added desserts and deli sandwiches to their product lineup, something the franchisor wouldn't allow. As independents, their sales are double what they were under the franchise umbrella. In retrospect, they say they should have researched the company more carefully. Judy maintains they weren't told the truth about the location's potential, and says they never made back their franchise fees.

Lawsuits between franchisor and franchisees are a sign of trouble. So is a large turnover in franchised outlets. If franchisees are going bankrupt, or selling their franchises, that's a sign that it's difficult to operate a profitable business with this organization.

"BUYER BEWARE"

Some franchisors stretch the truth about franchisees' potential profits. In particular, pro forma statements have to be taken with a grain of salt. Pro forma statements look like profit-and-loss statements, except they apply to a hypothetical future rather than to a concrete past. They're franchisors' claims about what can be achieved in a given location. You should determine whether projected sales and expenses are realistic. Do the statements take into account all expenses? Are staffing levels listed in the statement realistic? Are projected sales achievable? Are the rent charges accurate? It's a good idea to prepare your own projections, and seek comment from your accountant.

American franchisors operate under "franchise disclosure laws" that oblige them to divulge relevant information about fees, products, background and so on to potential franchisees. This obligation applies to U.S. companies operating in Canada. Alberta is the only Canadian province with franchise legislation. If you're dealing with an American or Alberta company, get its disclosure statement. The only law governing franchisors in other provinces is *caveat emptor*.

FRANCHISE AGREEMENTS

Franchise agreements are notoriously one-sided. And there is rarely room for negotiation. Theoretically, this protects both franchisors and franchisees, by protecting the organization against shoddy operators. Most agreements have termination clauses that can be invoked if the franchisee acts in such a way as to damage the franchisor's reputation or fails to observe company procedures by operating a dirty store or breaching trade marks, for example. Usually the franchisor will give a poorly performing franchisee notice to fix a problem, and terminate only if the problem persists. Franchisors will also terminate for failure to pay royalties or for filing false statements in the hope of evading royalty payments. If the franchise is terminated, the franchisee forfeits his or her franchise fee. The franchisor may buy back leasehold improvements, but usually they belong to the landlord. The franchisor may buy back inventory less a restocking charge. Franchise agreements are complex. Before signing an agreement, you should have it checked by a lawyer familiar with these documents. Sometimes agreements contain hidden charges, or are structured so that franchisees can never make back their franchise fee. "Not all franchisees are McDonald's," cautions Joe Miller, vice-president of the Federal Business Development Bank. "And it's getting worse."

Is Franchising Right for You?
Besides looking at the franchise system, the contract and the location, potential franchisees should also look at themselves. First of all, they should consider their willingness to operate within a tight system. A franchisee is part entrepreneur, part manager: entrepreneurial enough to go into business, but not someone who wants to change the system. It's fine to make suggestions and fine adjustments to suit local conditions, but they have to be made within the framework of the franchise system.

Judy says she may have been too entrepreneurial for the franchisee, but defends her approach. "Working down here, I knew what would work in the store. They felt their concept was right." She admits that too much innovation can ruin a franchise system. "If not controlled, some people might run crazy, and turn their store into a negative situation for the whole chain. But franchisees should be given a chance to adapt to their locations."

Is the Franchise Right for You?
Potential franchisees should also consider how well they like the concept. It's not unusual for an owner of a mall retail franchise location to put in 60-hour weeks, then do paperwork on Sundays.

Franchising has put thousands of Canadians in their own successful businesses. Bill and Judy's experience, and Laanep's, may not be typical. But they do illustrate some of the issues potential franchisees should address *before* they sign a contract.

RESEARCHING A NEW MARKET

Compared to buying an existing business or franchise, starting a new business has greater risks. But building a successful enterprise around a new idea also has greater rewards, both financial and psychological. Evaluating a new business opportunity is difficult, since you don't have a history on which to base your estimates. With a new business, estimating sales involves guesswork. (The same applies if you're planning radical changes to an existing business or expanding into a new field or location.) But it should be informed guesswork.

WHO'S THE COMPETITION?

For someone who has developed a new product or service, the first step is to do a literature search, says Ray Kong, manager of consulting services for the York Consulting Group. Affiliated with the faculty of administrative studies of York University of Toronto, the group helps new and existing companies conduct market research, prepare business plans, perform accounting and cashflow analysis and develop marketing strategy. Most of its clients are small businesses. "Is the product really new, or is someone already doing it?" Kong asks.

Trade magazines may provide an answer. So will general-interest periodicals. A fast way to get information is to use computerized databases such as Info Globe or Dialog, accessible to anyone with a personal computer and a modem. When you enter "keywords," these databases will list all the articles published on a given subject. If you're not an experienced computer user, there are research services that can conduct database searches for you. Some public libraries also perform this service. *The BOSS Directory*, published by the federal Department of Industry, Science and Technology, lists all Canadian companies by industry type. In addition to competitors, these information sources may also reveal suppliers and customers.

For companies with small local markets, simply walking or driving around and looking at local businesses may show you who your competitors are. Many municipalities conduct regular surveys of businesses in their regions. By calling your local planning department, you can find out the number of local companies serving your industry. Again, this source may also reveal potential customers and suppliers.

CAN YOU COMPETE?

Having identified your competitors, you have to evaluate them. Who are you up against? Do you have the resources to compete with them? Kong says it's valuable to consider indirect as well as direct competition. Airlines and railways are indirect competitors because both provide transportation services. Are there companies whose product or service, while different from yours, satisfies the same need?

WHO ARE YOUR CUSTOMERS?

You also have to identify the size of your market. To do that, you first have to identify your customers. Who's going to buy your product or service? In some cases, for example a store selling maternity clothing, this is absurdly simple. In other cases, it's more complex. You may have to make a deliberate decision about the portion of the market you plan to target. Once you've identified the market, it becomes easier to determine its size. From census data, Statistics Canada can provide valuable demographic information, such as average income, age, rate of home ownership, for a specific group. If you're selling maternity clothing, getting information about birth rates in your area will tell you a lot about the local market. You can get information free of charge at Stats Can libraries (if you want a Stats Can librarian to do the job for you, there will be a modest charge). The same information may be available from your municipal planning department. Ethnicity information—relevant if your business, like that of the Kokerams, is targeted to a specific ethnic group—is available from some planning departments.

Stats Can may also be able to provide information on sales in your product area. If you're planning to sell office equipment, for example, they could provide information about sales of FAX machines and copiers. Besides indicating the size of the market, this information can tell you whether a market's expanding or shrinking, and whether it represents a good *long-term* opportunity.

WHAT'S YOUR EDGE?

Next, take a hard look at your product. Why is your product better than the competition's? What will make someone buy it? You should also consider the possibility of a competitor's copying your idea and stealing your edge.

If you're selling an industrial product (that is, if the end-users are other businesses rather than individuals), getting the answer to these questions is easier than if you're selling a consumer product. Especially if you're selling to a narrow, specialized market, you can get opinions from your end-users. Would they be willing to buy the product? For what price? Can you make a profit at that price?

DO PEOPLE WANT TO BUY YOUR PRODUCT?

If you're selling a consumer product, it's much harder to get opinions from end-users because there are so many of them. There are several ways of doing market research. You can conduct a survey of people who represent your target market. This can accomplish two things: it can show whether people want your product, and it can provide valuable insights into the kind of product they want. Some entrepreneurs do consumer research by discussing their product with family and friends. While this method can provide valuable input, it has two great weaknesses, according to Ronald Rotenberg, associate professor of marketing at Brock University in St. Catharines, Ontario. First, friends and family are probably biased in favour of your product, so won't provide critical comment. Second, they represent a small sample, which may not be representative of your market. It may be valuable to have a "focus group" of informed individuals to help identify your product's strengths and weaknesses, as long as they're sufficiently critical.

SURVEYS

For a new consumer product, you want to conduct a scientific survey of randomly chosen individuals. This can be expensive and time-consuming, but it's a lot cheaper than launching a business based on an unsellable concept. Usually, 300 to 400 respondents are needed for a survey to be statistically valid, but meaningful information can be gleaned from a survey of 100 people. Rotenberg, who operates a market research company, says the cost of a straightforward survey of 100 people ranges from $2,500 to $5,000. With samples of 300 to 400, costs range from $5,000 to $10,000. Surveys of specialized markets cost more because of the difficulty in getting respondents.

While it's possible to conduct these studies yourself, developing questionnaires and screening respondents is a specialized task, and it takes more time than many entrepreneurs can spare. Hence, many turn to market-research firms. In addition to providing expertise and saving time, using a research firm may add credibility to your financing proposal. As Kong notes, lenders will take claims about market size and probable market share more seriously if they're endorsed by an independent third party. However, you should make sure the firm understands your business and product.

Besides confirming that there's a market for your product, surveys and focus groups can provide valuable insights about the kind of product your market wants.

Russell Knight, associate professor of entrepreneurship at the University of Western Ontario's school of business administration, suggests businesses seek opinions about their product's chances for success before embarking on expensive and time-consuming consumer studies. If you're planning to sell automotive accessories, talk to hardware and automotive stores. "If they say no, you might as well quit."

THE "OBSERVATION METHOD"

Observation is another alternative. Instead of asking questions, you directly observe consumer behaviour, record it and analyse it. For this method to work, you have to know what you're looking for, Rotenberg notes. And it's not always practical. But sometimes it can yield valuable insights.

Joe Miller tells of an entrepreneur who was offered a space for a fast-food restaurant in an indoor mall. Based on the landlord's claims about traffic and potential sales, the location looked promising. However, he decided to do some first-hand research himself. "He took a common-sense approach," Miller relates. "He went to the mall and counted customers. He looked at the price range of what they were buying, and figured out his achievable sales. As it turned out, the figures from the mall landlord were way out of whack, and he decided not to take the location."

IS IT FEASIBLE?

Your market research should tell you whether people want to buy your product and what they're willing to pay for it. The next step is to determine whether you can produce it at that price. You have to estimate the portion of the market you can capture, and your likely revenues, and compare revenues with costs. Projecting revenues may be a matter of predicting the number of sales you'll make on a daily, weekly or monthly basis, then multiplying that by the dollar value of an average sale. For a fast-food restaurant, that might be $5; for an upscale dress shop, $200. Given seasonal variations, you'll have to do projections for each week or month. Subtracting revenues from expenses will tell you if your venture is feasible. These are just projections, remember. "There's a lot of judgment involved," Kong comments. "A lot of business planning comes down to estimating."

At some point, you're going to have to make a "leap of faith." It's one thing to identify the size of your market; it's another to predict the share you can take. It's one thing to identify the individuals or companies who are potential customers for your product. It's another to say how many will actually buy your product. Even consumer surveys won't give a firm answer. Putting hard-earned cash on the counter is quite different from telling a survey-taker you'd buy a product. As Knight notes, "You never really know if there's a market for your product till you open your doors. Actual selling is the only real test."

A thorough evaluation of your business opportunity doesn't guarantee success, but it makes the likelihood of success much greater. As the refrain "I should have done more research" shows, evaluating the business opportunity is a vital task that, all too often, is not done well enough. Moreover, scrutinizing your business opportunity carefully often reveals useful answers about how best to address it. That's the function of a business plan, a topic we'll explore in the next chapter.

3/PLANNING FOR SUCCESS:
The Business Plan and Related Documents

If Graham Edwards's Indianapolis 500 board game makes him a
millionaire, it won't be by accident. He's spent years planning every
aspect of his new venture. It started in September 1984, when he and
a friend were playing Scrabble while watching an auto race on TV.
The idea of a board game based on auto-racing occurred to them.

Edwards continued to work part time as a musician and freelance
writer while researching the market. He contacted the Molson and
Labatt breweries (both of which sponsor Canadian auto races), the
Indianapolis Motor Speedway, Championship Auto Racing Teams
(CART, the sanctioning body for auto racing), and a Swiss
public-relations firm that arranges racing-team sponsorships. Using
information from these sources, he was able to determine the average
age of racing audiences, their average income, education, the products
and services they use, recent major purchases, spending habits and
other important information.

That information was vital. First of all, it told Edwards that there
was a market for his game. Race-day attendance at the Indy 500 is
500,000; another 50 million watch the event on TV. And the
spectators are well-heeled. Edwards's research told him that 40
percent of auto-racing fans have a university education—a high
proportion—and that their average annual income is more than
US $35,000. The research also showed Edwards the audience for
which he ought to develop his game. "We faced a decision on how
complex the game ought to be, whether it should be a game for racing
fans or for everyone. Our objective was to make it interesting for
fans, and enjoyable for their friends."

Having confirmed there was a market, Edwards had to determine
how he would address it. From mid-1985 until spring 1986, he
worked full time to develop a business plan for his enterprise,

Toronto-based Games International Inc. The plan addressed every challenge his company would face: developing the game, hiring artists, manufacturing the games, marketing them, distributing them, managing his company, getting financing.

The work paid some early dividends. After nine months of negotiation, he was able to secure the rights to produce the official board game of the Indianapolis auto race. Games International wasn't the only company negotiating with the Speedway. "There are other large U.S. games companies who wanted the licence," Edwards recalls. How was a small Canadian startup able to out-manoeuvre large, established American competitors? By doing its homework. "The Speedway knew that whomever they licensed would be dealing with its reputation," he notes. "They liked our game and they liked our marketing strategies."

Edwards's legwork was critical in getting financing. "Without assurance to potential investors and bankers that I had done my homework, financial backing would have been impossible to obtain." He's raised $100,000 by liquidating everything he owns, and through loans from friends and the bank. In early 1989, he sold half the company in return for $200,000, which will let him buy artwork and put the game into production.

But he also has ambitious promotion plans, which include print ads using real Indy drivers, elaborate store displays and exhibits of real Indy cars in shopping centres. Total budget for advertising and public relations is $1.2 million, which Edwards plans to raise by selling spaces on game cards or the game board to firms that sponsor races or racing teams. These include oil companies, auto makers, auto-products companies, computer firms, hotel chains, airlines and credit-card companies. His early research is proving critical, since he knows which products and services racing fans buy.

Edwards has covered every aspect of his venture, from concept and design to distribution and marketing. By the time his game hits retail shelves in late 1989, five years will have elapsed. That may seem a long time to spend planning a venture; but then Edwards is expecting a handsome reward. "I hope to sell one million games over the next four years. If I do, it will make me a millionaire. That won't mean as much as the satisfaction that success would bring. As nice as the money would be, it's the doing of it that counts the most."

PLANNING YOUR BUSINESS

Not all new businesses spend as much time as Games International before they're ready to market their product. In fact, as Toronto businessman Peter Cook notes, you can overanalyse a business opportunity. Cook, who lectures on entrepreneurship at Centennial College in Scarborough, Ontario, says he started a temporary-help agency for retired business people after researching the market for two weeks. His first business, a Montreal home-repair and renovation agency, took four months to plan.

Regardless of how long it takes, this planning stage is vital. Once you've decided to go ahead with your business, you have to set goals and determine how you'll achieve them. It's not sufficient to work this out in your head. In order to obtain financing, you have to get it down on paper. The document that outlines the company's goals and strategies is called the "business plan." Your accountant can help you develop a business plan, and evaluate it once it's finished.

You can be sure that potential investors and lenders will ask tough questions about your plans. With a well-researched business plan, you'll be able to answer them. It will show lenders and investors that there's a market for your product, that the product is competitive, that your business's management is qualified, that it has adequate physical and financial resources to create the product—in short, that your company represents a good risk.

Also, preparing a business plan forces you to think about the challenges you'll face in your business. That way, you won't be surprised when they come. And you'll be able to take advance action to minimize their impact. You'll be able to develop your business following a preconceived game plan, rather than improvising as you go along. As happened with Edwards, information gathered during the planning stage may help you fine-tune your product.

PREPARING A BUSINESS PLAN

The content and structure of a business plan will vary from business to business. A retailer's business plan, for example, needs to address location carefully. A manufacturer's must address production issues. But there are many common elements.

Generally, the plan will start with a brief introduction to the company, outlining its objectives, its products and their advantages, its market, its management, its financial outlook. If the plan is being used to obtain financing, the introduction should indicate the amount and type of financing required, and tell how the money will be spent. The rest of the plan should explore these issues in greater detail.

MANAGEMENT

Your business plan should include executive profiles for the entire management team, listing experience, abilities, aptitudes and references. Outline any accomplishments that demonstrate a team member's ability to perform his or her duties. Lenders and investors want to be sure management has essential financial, production and marketing skills. If your team is weak in any area, show how you plan to address these weaknesses. Will you recruit the help you need? Retain outside consultants? Train internal people? The duties and remuneration packages of key managers should be outlined. If appropriate, an organizational chart should be included. This section should also spell out the participation of all the shareholders, outlining their monetary and non-monetary contributions to the firm.

EMPLOYEES

Staffing requirements should also be addressed. You should indicate the functions employees will perform, and the skills they'll need to perform them. Outline the methods you'll use to train employees: on-the-job, manufacturers' courses or outside seminars. Specify current and future wages; and compare them with those paid by competitors and other companies in the area. If your operation is unionized, discuss your plans for dealing with the union. Particularly in tough labour markets, such as Southern Ontario, you should consider how you plan to attract staff. If you plan to use technology to improve productivity, you should include this in your business plan. The same applies to any plans you have to minimize turnover and absenteeism.

If you have experience in the industry you're planning to enter, you may already know the answers to some of these questions. Your local Canada Employment and Immigration Centre should be able to provide information about local labour supply and wage rates. Industry associations can often provide more detailed information about the labour situation in your business. Business people in your area and industry are another source of information. In any event, don't blithely assume you'll be able to meet your staff requirements. As we'll see in Chapter 7, obtaining staff will be one of the greatest challenges you will face in the 1990s.

YOUR PRODUCT

Lenders and investors want to know what distinguishes your product. Your business plan should describe your products or services in layman's terms, and explain their advantages over competing products. Brochures, photographs or sketches will help get the message across. Outline your products' key features and benefits, and compare them with those of your competitors. Be frank about your product's limitations. Outline the ways in which your product is protected from competition, for example, patents, copyrights, trade secrets, exclusive distribution arrangements or long lead time between product conception and delivery.

If your product isn't ready for market, describe the research and development activities necessary to get it to that stage. Estimate how much time and money you'll have to spend before you have a prototype and before you go into production. If you have competitors, compare your situation with theirs. Also, outline the regulatory-approval requirements governing your product. And discuss plans for future products.

YOUR MARKET

For this area of your business plan, you'll have done a lot of preparatory work when you determined the feasibility of your venture. Its purpose is to show that there's a market for your product or service, that your product meets its customers' needs and that the market can be served profitably.

Include information about market trends. What's the size of the market? Is it growing, shrinking or stagnant? Where will it be in one year, five years, ten years? Will the market be affected by technological developments or changing customer needs? Does your product address a brand-new market? If so, is the market ready for your product?

If there are other companies in your market, who are they? Why is there room for another supplier? What portion of the market do you think you can take from competitors? How will you take it? Does your product have features competing products lack? Is it priced more aggressively? Is your service better? Is your location better? How are your competitors likely to respond, and how will you react to their responses? What are your competitors' strengths and weaknesses? Compare their management skills in finance, operations and marketing with your own. Investors or lenders want to know what your advantage over competitors—your "edge"—is, and whether you can sustain it.

As with all areas of your business plan, your market studies are only as good as the information on which they're based. Industry associations can provide information about the size and growth of the market for your product. Trade magazines often publish statistics on the markets they cover. Most editors have hectic schedules, but many will talk to you for a few minutes. In that time, they may be able to provide valuable insights on your market. Suppliers are necessarily familiar with the markets they serve; and indirectly, your market is their market. All the information sources listed in Chapter 2 for market research apply here.

MARKETING PLANS

In your market research, you should identify the people who are going to buy your product. If you know such characteristics as age, sex and income of your target market, you'll be able to focus your marketing efforts more precisely. Who's going to buy your products? Why do they buy the kind of product you're making? How often do they buy it? What factors most influence purchase decisions: price, location, features, service? How loyal are they to competitors' products? Who makes the purchase decisions? How do they respond to advertising?

You should also outline your pricing policy, and indicate the contribution each product makes toward your company's profits. Compare your pricing policy with that of your competitors, and show how yours will help you obtain market share while making a profit. Estimate the sales and market share you need to survive and grow; and compare that with the volumes you think you can achieve in each of your first five years of business. If you have firm commitments for your product, identify them.

Next, outline the steps you'll take to meet your sales goals. Describe the distribution methods you'll use to sell your product. Will you use distributors? A direct sales force? A retail network? How will the sales force be recruited? How will it be compensated? Estimate the efficiency of your sales network: the size of the average order and the number of calls it will take to obtain an order.

You should also discuss the methods you'll use to generate awareness of your product. Do you plan to use advertising? In what media? What about other promotional vehicles, such as tradeshows, public relations and direct mail? What will these promotions cost? Describe how your promotional plans are suitable for the groups you've identified as your target market. Again, you should compare your sales and promotion plans with those of your competitors, noting their strengths and weaknesses.

Data for sales costs should be available from your industry association. The association may be able to help you determine promotional costs as well, though advertising agencies and sales reps for the media you plan to use are more likely sources for this information. We'll discuss marketing in more detail in Chapter 8, "Dealing with Customers."

OPERATIONS

In this section, you explain how you'll produce whatever it is you're selling. You should describe the location and its advantages. Obviously, this is crucial for a retail operation, but it's important for any kind of business. How close is your location to customers? To suppliers? To transportation? What are the costs of the location, such as rent, local taxes and utilities? Will you lease or buy the premises, or perhaps share them with another business? Does the building suit your needs? Is there adequate storage and parking space? Will your activities be restricted by local laws or lease requirements?

What equipment and fixtures will you need? What will it cost? Will you rent, lease or buy the equipment? Will you have to make building improvements, such as upgraded electrical service, to become operational? What will all this cost? How will your needs change in the future as your company grows? We'll deal with these issues in greater detail in Chapter 5, "Location, Location, Location."

This section should also include a description of the processes used to manufacture your product or perform your service; and the advantages of your processes over competitors'. Analyse the cost of your processes, and separate fixed costs (such as mortgage payments) from variable costs (such as raw materials). Outline which materials you'll make yourself, and which you'll buy. Show how much your production capacity can grow to accommodate increasing demand.

List potential suppliers of materials, components and resale goods, and contractors that will perform essential services. You should be aware of their credit terms, delivery schedules, distribution rights and requirements and promotion support. Also, indicate your transportation needs, and the cost of meeting them.

Your personal experience will probably give some of the answers to these questions. You can get information on building locations from municipal governments. Information on processes, equipment and materials can be obtained from suppliers.

TIMING

List the most important tasks you have to address in your new business in the next three to five years. These might include development of a prototype, finding premises, hiring key staff, purchasing equipment, going into production and launching your product. Be realistic. It's easy to underestimate the time required.

FINANCE

To obtain financing, you'll need financial statements and projections for the next three to five years. (If you're financing an existing business, you'll need statements for past years as well.) The first of these is a financial forecast. Essentially, this is a "crystal-ball" profit-and-loss statement; that is, it applies to a hypothetical future rather than to the concrete past. The projection summarizes the financial data you've collected and shows the income you expect. Subtracting the cost of goods sold (materials, labour and factory overhead) from sales will indicate projected gross profit. Factory overhead includes such items as rent, repairs and maintenance, utilities, depreciation on machinery and amortization of leasehold improvements. Net pre-tax profit is obtained by subtracting selling expenses, general and administrative expenses and financial expenses from gross profit. Sales expenses include commissions, travel, shipping, advertising and automobile operating costs plus depreciation. Administrative expenses include office and administrative salaries, insurance, telephone, printing and stationery and depreciation on furniture and fixtures. Show which costs are fixed—that is, costs that remain constant regardless of sales—and which are variable—those that vary with sales. Fixed costs might include rent or payments on loans for equipment. Variable costs might include sales commissions.

You'll also need a forecast balance sheet and cashflow projections covering the same periods as your income projections. On the debit or "plus" side, the balance sheet will list current assets, such as cash and bank accounts, accounts receivable, inventory and pre-paid expenses, and fixed assets, such as land and buildings, fixtures and equipment, automobiles and leasehold improvements (less depreciation). On the credit or "minus" side, it will list liabilities, which will consist of current debt (accounts payable, taxes payable, demand loans and the current portion of long-term debt) and long-term debt (mortgages and shareholder loans). The difference between assets and liabilities is net worth or equity. The difference between current assets and liabilities indicates the working-capital requirements of the business, the amount you'll need from the bank in addition to term loans or equity used to finance fixed assets. (For more on different types of bank loans, see Chapter 4, "Startup Financing.")

To do a cashflow projection, you list projected cash receipts and disbursements on a month-by-month basis. In most retail operations (except those with in-house charging privileges), sales come in as cash. But many businesses grant trade credit to customers, so they may not collect for 60 to 90 days after a sale is made. In the meantime, they have to cover expenses. The cashflow projection will show, for any given month, whether cash disbursements will exceed receipts, and thus the business's cash shortfall or receipts will exceed disbursements. (We'll discuss financial statements and projections in greater detail in Chapter 6, "Managing Money.")

You'll also need net-worth statements for all shareholders in the business. This statement lists assets such as home, cottage, car, stocks and bonds, deposits, insurance policies, and liabilities, such as mortgages and loans. The difference between the two is net worth.

FINANCING REQUIREMENTS

In this section, you tell how much money you need now, and how it will be used. You should also indicate what you'll do if you've underestimated your cash requirements. Outline your plans for obtaining necessary financing, whether through bank loans, government loans or grants, assistance from family or friends or outside investors, mortgaging your home, surrendering or borrowing on insurance policies, or securing trade credit. If you're borrowing money, outline the expected terms and how you intend to pay it back. If you're looking for investors, outline plans, such as public share offerings or mergers, whereby investors will be able to get their money out of the company.

COVERING ALL THE BASES

Your business plan should be written in non-technical language, so that readers unfamiliar with your industry can understand the document. At the same time, it should be thorough. It should give readers a detailed picture of your industry and your business.

It should be well documented. To maintain credibility with lenders and investors, back up your statements and list your sources of information. Be frank about the risk involved in your business. On some points—your projected market share, for example—you'll probably have to rely on gut feel rather than hard fact. Make sure the reader knows this.

Because some projections are necessarily based on gut feel, actual performance can vary widely. Sometimes forecasts turn out to be accurate. Often they're not. Sales projections can be very accurate if a business already has sales commitments before opening. In other cases, especially when making a new product without sales commitments, they can be quite inaccurate.

Sales are one side of financial projections. The other side is expenses, which most new businesses underestimate. Often, they fail to account for significant expenses, such as business taxes. A small retail store might have to pay $1,000 to $1,500 a year, depending on where it's located. In addition, it's common to underestimate expenses one does account for, particularly staff.

Many new businesses overlook marketing, adds Russell Knight, associate professor at the University of Western Ontario's school of business administration. For his class on entrepreneurship, Knight brings in entrepreneurs who have been in business for a couple of years. Students discuss the initial business plan, then the entrepreneur recounts what actually happened. Usually, the reality is quite different from the initial plan.

For one thing, new businesses are often unprepared for high marketing expenses. "Often, they have not considered how the world will know about their product," Knight comments. And often, they don't realize how hard it will be to get the business off the ground. "It can take double or triple the amount of money and time expected. If they're started on a shoestring, the odds are they're going to fail."

Adds Joe Miller, vice-president and Ontario regional general manager for the Federal Business Development Bank: "You should observe the rule of conservative accounting: underbudget revenue and overbudget expenses. You probably won't be conservative enough. We've hardly ever had anyone forecast a loss for year one. But 90 percent of companies do lose money in their first year." The combination of lower-than-expected sales and higher-than-expected expenses means some new businesses exhaust their working capital. With a more solid foundation, these businesses might survive.

To avoid this problem, entrepreneurs should develop financial projections for a range of sales. This will show their businesses' sensitivity to sales levels, that is, their viability should sales not grow as quickly as anticipated. Performing this kind of analysis should make it easier to get financing.

Developing this information significantly improves your chances of success. Knowing your break-even scenario puts you in a position to improve it. By cutting expenses, you can put your venture in a position to tolerate lower sales. You might rent half of a building, with the option to take over the other half if sales justify it. You might defer buying machinery till half-way through your first fiscal year, and rent instead.

The goal is to segment variable costs, which can be cut when sales are low, from fixed costs, which must be paid regardless of sales. If you've borrowed money to purchase expensive equipment, the debt must be serviced regardless of sales. If you've rented the equipment, the monthly payment will probably be higher than the cost of the loan. But depending on the rental agreement, you should be able to return the equipment if sales are lower than anticipated. Or perhaps you can turn to outside services instead of buying equipment up front.

Many new businesses are too ambitious, Knight agrees. "If someone's invented a widget, maybe they should subcontract manufacturing from someone better equipped, and concentrate on marketing and delivery in the early stages. Everyone wants to make their own product; but it might be better to wait until the product is established and funding is in place."

As we've seen, there are a lot of angles to cover in a business plan. You'll almost certainly need help from your accountant with the financial projections; and you may wish to retain an outside consultant for other areas.

With a well-researched business plan, you'll have considered the major challenges you'll face in your own business. And you'll be ready to confront your first challenge: getting financing. We'll discuss that in the next chapter. One final word: your business plan and supporting documents will contain vital information about your business. Show them only to those people who need to know about your venture: lenders and potential investors. If there's a possibility investors may be in contact with your competitors, consider having them sign a non-disclosure agreement.

4/ STARTUP FINANCING:
Getting the Money You Need

If Greg Pastic had listened to the first banker he approached for startup financing, he might be shuffling paper for the government instead of presiding over a $2-million-a-year business. A Toronto native, Pastic had spent a couple of years working in Sweden. One of his employers was a classical-record producer. Soon after Pastic returned to Toronto in 1979, the firm suggested he act as its Canadian distributor. It would pay for shipping, and would take records back if Pastic was unable to sell them. After Pastic sold the first shipment to local record shops, two other Swedish record labels approached him.

To finance inventory, Pastic needed money. He put together an outline of his business—the product, the market and his sales so far—and approached his local bank manager for a $3,000 term loan. Pastic's family had been dealing with that branch for 20 years, and he had had two personal loans, which he'd repaid on schedule.

"Greg, it doesn't sound like a good idea to me," the manager chided. "Think about your future. Why don't you get a good civil-service job, where you can get yourself a nice pension?" Pastic was discouraged. "I didn't go to him for advice, I went for money," he recalls.

But instead of giving up, Pastic vowed to prove the bank manager wrong. He asked his suppliers for extended terms. A reference from Pastic's former Swedish employer helped persuade the other labels to give him 90 days instead of 30 days to pay for shipments. Working a couple of days a week, he managed to sell $25,000 worth of records during his first year in business. Because of setup costs, he had a small loss.

Within a year, opportunities arose to distribute classical-record labels from other countries. To do this, Pastic needed financing, and decided to approach a different bank. This time, he was better prepared. He and his accountant put together a detailed business plan, which they presented to the second manager. She granted a $10,000 loan.

Pastic's persistence paid off handsomely. Scandinavian Record Import Ltd. (SRI) distributes more than a dozen different labels of classical-music recordings from the United States, Britain and Europe, making it the largest independent classical-record distributor in Canada. In fiscal 1988, SRI had after-tax profits of $260,000 on sales of $2 million. Now based in Peterborough, Ontario, the company employs seven people full time.

Pastic acknowledges that luck and timing had a lot to do with his success. After the compact disc was launched in 1983, classical-music buffs took to the new medium with wild abandon; and SRI's sales exploded. Pastic had no idea this would happen when he started his business. But if he'd listened to that first bank manager, he'd have missed this opportunity.

FUNDING SOURCES

Getting financing is the first major hurdle new businesses face. The initial challenge—evaluating the opportunity and putting the right team together—are certainly formidable. But they're more or less under the budding entrepreneur's control. Once you've researched your market, either you go ahead with the business or you don't. But getting startup financing involves persuading a stranger to lend or invest money in your idea. Once you've presented your proposal, the decision is in someone else's hands.

Pastic acknowledges that he didn't help himself as much as he could have. For one thing, he approached a consumer banker rather than a commercial one. Still, instead of referring Pastic to a business lender, the manager discouraged him. Also, Pastic wasn't prepared for the manager's tough questions on his proposal: how he would address the marketing, finance and operational challenges he'd inevitably face. "I'm a person who looks at an opportunity, and if it's within my capabilities, I tackle it," Pastic explains. "It boils down to being a good judge without overanalysing an issue."

Almost always, you'll need some equity in your business—money you've invested or are prepared to invest in your venture. Sources include savings, securities, equity in your home and cash surrender-value of life insurance policies. You can either sell or borrow against these securities to obtain equity for your business. Some entrepreneurs go as far as getting cash advances on credit cards to obtain funds for their businesses. Bear in mind that personal debt will have to be serviced. You may be unable to draw a salary for a while after opening your business, or your salary may be small.

"Love money" – financial assistance from relatives and friends – is a common source of startup funding for new businesses. But borrowing money from friends and family can bring severe tensions into otherwise healthy relationships, especially if the loans aren't repaid on time. Sometimes the mere request for financial assistance is enough to strain a relationship.

APPLYING FOR A LOAN

Regardless of how they obtain equity, most new businesses need outside financing to get going. That involves either borrowing money from a bank or other lender or attracting other investors for your business. The amount lending institutions will advance varies "all over the map," says Joe Miller, vice-president and Ontario regional general manager for the Federal Business Development Bank (FBDB). But as a rough rule of thumb, you'll be able to borrow a maximum of 50 percent of the startup costs of your business; that is, you'll need a debt-to-equity ratio of at least 50 percent. Lenders expect borrowers to put up half the cost of starting the business for several reasons. For one thing, the fact the borrower is willing to risk a substantial amount of money indicates his or her seriousness about the business. For another, the more the borrower invests, the less exposed the lender is should the business fail. Also, the less money borrowed, the less the business will be weighed down by interest charges.

Lenders carefully will consider the individual making the application, but they also want to evaluate the business proposal. They want to be assured that applicants are aware of the challenges facing them, and know how they're going to address them. Bear in mind that banks don't like rejecting applications; they derive the majority of their revenue from commercial loans. But they want to make sure borrowers can service the loan and repay the principal – hence the scrutiny to which they subject loan applications.

SHOPPING FOR A BANK
There are several things an applicant can do to improve his or her

chances. First of all, shop around for a lender. If possible, deal with a commercial rather than consumer branch. Canada's major chartered banks maintain independent business centres to address the needs of small- and medium-sized businesses.

Unlike corporate banking centres, which offer sophisticated cash-management programs, independent business centres offer products geared to small business, such as government-guaranteed small-business loans, consolidated accounts for payroll and other applications, and life insurance to protect company loans. The main difference between corporate and small-business banking needs is that, because small businesses usually lack in-house financial expertise, they rely more heavily on bankers and accountants.

If there isn't an independent business centre in your area, try to find a large branch operated by a senior manager. A manager at a small neighbourhood branch, like the one Pastic first approached, will usually have a small discretionary spending limit. Loans above this limit must be referred to regional or head office. Ideally, the manager will have some experience in dealing with your industry.

Types of Loans
When applying for financing, it's important to know what kind of loan you want. *Term loans*, repaid over a fixed period of time, are used to finance long-term assets such as equipment and vehicles. The period of the loan will be related to the expected useful life of the assets. You can't finance equipment that will be obsolete or worn out in five years over a seven-year period. *Mortgage loans* are used to finance expensive assets with a long life, such as land and buildings.

Operating loans are used to finance fluctuating assets such as receivables and inventory. Usually, banks will lend 60 to 75 percent of the value of the inventory of receivables, but require that these assets be assigned to the bank. To provide this service, also known as a *line of credit*, banks need to get aged receivable listings each month. These show the amount of money owed to the business, and how long the money has been outstanding. They may also require quarterly listings of aged accounts payable and inventory. You draw on your line of credit when you need money, and pay interest on the amount you withdraw. You'll be able to access your line of credit in pre-fixed increments, usually $1,000 or so. Many banks will automatically access the line as your account requires, and will pay down the debt when there's enough money in your account. Once you've exhausted your line of credit, the bank will start returning cheques. As we'll see below, banks are reluctant to grant small operating loans because of the cost of administering them.

When applying, present your case clearly and enthusiastically. Make sure the manager is familiar with your personal strengths, and your company's. The best way to do this is to develop a written financing proposal. This should include a personal résumé and financial statement, your business and financial plans, as well as supporting documentation outlined in the last chapter. The proposal should spell out how much money is required, how it will be used and how you intend to repay it. It should describe your business, its products and clients, its plant and staff. The proposal should be written clearly and concisely, using non-technical language. Expect to be grilled about every detail of your proposal.

SUPPORTING DOCUMENTS

When all documents accompany the loan application, it typically takes 10 working days to get an answer, says Gerry LeJan, manager of the Royal Bank of Canada's independent business centre in downtown Toronto. Often, however, applicants fail to prepare cashflow projections or statements of personal net worth. Usually the bank will ask them to provide this information, lengthening the application process. Having this information is important for the bank and the business, LeJan notes. Without a cashflow projection, the business is unaware of its real funding needs. If it comes back to the bank a few months later, the bank is in a dilemma. Is the money needed because the applicant underestimated his or her requirements or because the business is in trouble?

If you're turned down at first, remember Pastic's experience. Try to determine the reasons for the rejection. They may have little to do with the viability of your business. For example, the bank manager may already have made several loans to businesses in your particular industry and may be reluctant to expose the bank to a downturn in your industry. If necessary, revise your proposal, then approach another lender whose outlook and background are better suited to your situation.

LENDING CRITERIA: THE "FOUR Cs"

CHARACTER

LeJan says lenders use a formula called the "four Cs" to evaluate business applications. *Character* is the first test LeJan applies to a loan application. "I want to know the character of the individual on the other side of the desk, and their company," he explains. "Have they been bankrupt before? Is there a pattern of them suing or being sued? That can tell you something about the mentality of the person. What's the individual's background? If the company is already in business, what's its reputation?"

CAPACITY

The next criterion is the *capacity* of the business to do what it says it will do. That's why the business plan is so vital. "Often it will involve an individual without all the expertise required for the business," LeJan explains. "That's not critical if it's allowed for in the business plan. If the company is involved in manufacturing, I want to know if it has the capacity to produce the volumes indicated in the plan. I want to know if it has a sales force to market the product. I want to know if it has the cashflow to service the debt."

CONDITIONS

Lenders also consider *conditions* that affect the viability of the company. These factors include interest rates, labour supply, barriers to market entry, competition, any condition outside the owner/manager's control that may affect the success of the operation. They too should be addressed in the business plan.

It's not unusual to get outside assistance from an accountant or other professional in preparing a business plan. And it's not unusual for the accountant to sit in on meetings with lenders. But the entrepreneur should carry the ball from there. "You should understand the plan from cover to cover," advises Joe Miller of the FBDB. "Don't have your accountant explain it to the bank. They're lending to you. They want to know that the stakeholder knows what's going on."

Half the time spent evaluating the application will be devoted to analysing the numbers in the business plan, and the assumptions behind them, LeJan says. If an applicant predicts that margins will go up in the second year of operation, he wants to know why. For example, the product may be marketed as a loss-leader in year one to drum up business. The other half of the time is spent evaluating the venture itself: the product, the market, the plans of the company, the people behind it and the conditions that will affect it. "We'd like to know how an applicant got the idea, and the expertise to carry it out.

Maybe he worked in his family's business, then went to school to learn the mechanical processes used in it; and now has an idea for a different design." If the idea involves a political or moral hot potato, say importing goods from South Africa or operating an abortion clinic, lenders may decide not to participate, LeJan adds.

COLLATERAL

The last of the four Cs is *collateral.* "An applicant should think about what he's prepared to offer the bank as security," LeJan comments. "It may be corporate assets such as inventory, receivables, equipment and buildings. Or it may involve personal guarantees or mortgages on personal property. Or it may involve another guarantor.

"We want a back door if the product doesn't sell," he explains. "We may only be able to get 50 or 60 cents on the dollar for equipment. With a failed company, it may be impossible to collect receivables or sell inventory. So we might need another way out, say a mortgage. If everything works, collateral remains a non-issue; but it's our back door out of the thing. That is, if there's a shortfall in the first three Cs, collateral may increase our comfort level.

"If the venture doesn't look sound, we may not finance it regardless of the security. We're not in business to sell real estate, equipment or inventory. But we do some deals without security. All four Cs are equally important."

THE DOWNSIDE OF BANKS

Critics of Canada's banking system say lenders tend to stress collateral to the exclusion of other factors. The Canadian Federation of Independent Business (CFIB), a Toronto-based organization that represents 80,000 small and medium businesses, conducts an annual survey of members' concerns. A major concern is financing. According to Catherine Swift, the CFIB's chief economist and vice-president, members say banks' credit terms are becoming increasingly onerous—not just collateral, but also interest rates and service charges. This affects not only new, but expanding businesses.

"Banks in this country are basically collateral lenders," Swift comments. "If you put up security, you'll get the money. They don't lend on the basis of the business at all. Despite talk of cashflow, track record and character, collateral is 99 percent of the game." Firms under a year old are typically required to offer $5 collateral for every dollar lent, she maintains. The collateral-to-loan ratio for the total sample in the CFIB's 1988 survey was 2.7:1.

Banks are becoming less responsive to the needs of small business, she adds. "The guy who needs $5 million is better off than the guy who needs $30,000. For small transactions, banks are trying to make personal instead of business loans." And she says banks do not perform the advisory role they once did. "Bankers used to know their business customers; now it's an assembly-line operation."

LeJan says the reason banks don't provide as much service as small-business customers might like is cost. "It can take as much time to look after a $15,000 loan as a $100,000 loan. Banks are the same as retailers: they look after their big clients first. But we try to assure that our costs bear some relation to the benefits. Therefore small businesses may not get full-fledged account management. Instead we may set up a term loan."

With small loans, it doesn't pay to monitor receivables and inventory monthly, which banks normally do with operating loans. Paying $75 to $100 a month for an account manager to monitor the assets of a small business is "ludicrous," LeJan explains. "We'd prefer to give the customer the money and take something else as security—a house, car, personal guarantees, securities—especially if we're dealing with a very new business. We'll give the money over a three-year term, and let him manage his own account." LeJan suggests moving surplus funds into interest-bearing accounts and repaying the loan in large increments to avoid service charges.

Criticism of the banks' service to the small-business sector can be attributed to a misunderstanding of the banks' role, LeJan maintains. "Maybe we don't explain our role well enough: to provide funds to businesses with a better-than-average chance of succeeding. We're not venture capitalists. We deal with the fact that the entrepreneur has done something before, or that a product has been tried before. We're not in business to go out on a limb with every new idea, whether or not it's well-researched. We can't take excessive risks with shareholders' and depositors' money."

ALTERNATIVES

Entrepreneurs whose applications have been rejected by two or more conventional banks can turn to the Federal Business Development Bank, a federal agency whose mandate is to act as a "lender of last resort" for Canadian businesses. Because of the higher-risk nature of its business, the FBDB charges 1 to 2 percent more for its loans than do chartered banks. It still screens applications vigorously. "We're not giving out grants," explains Miller. "We're required to make a profit." The bank will lend money to viable firms whose needs can't be met by conventional lenders. A tourist camp in an isolated area might be viable, but might not have security to offer a bank. An urban manufacturer might need a longer term to pay off an equipment loan than a regular bank can offer. "This doesn't mean the deal isn't good, just that a conventional lender won't do it," Miller comments.

Banks are an important source of financing for small business, and a banking relationship is necessary for any business. But banks aren't the only source of funds. Indeed, before even approaching a bank, startup businesses should look into other sources of financing.

GOVERNMENT ASSISTANCE

Your business may qualify for government assistance: a grant, guaranteed loan or tax concessions. Across Canada, there are more than 10,000 different federal, provincial and municipal assistance programs for business. Some of these programs involve financial assistance. Others offer specific services to business, such as technology transfer.

The FBDB lists these programs in a series of books entitled *Assistance to Business in Canada*. A different volume is published for each province. These programs are also contained in the FBDB's Automated Information for Management (AIM) computer database. There is no charge for searching the database. People using the service describe their businesses to an operator, who conducts the search. A printout, listing programs for which the business may qualify, is given to the client.

A startup manufacturer in Northern Ontario, for example, might qualify for a business-improvement loan of up to $100,000 under the Small Business Loans Act (SBLA), administered by Industry, Science and Technology Canada (ISTC). SBLA loans, under which ISTC shares risk with a conventional lender, can be used by companies with annual sales under $2 million involved in communications, construction, fishing, manufacturing, retail, wholesaling, transportation and some service businesses to purchase premises or equipment. The business might also qualify for Canada Employment and Immigration's Job Development program, which subsidizes the wages of people who were previously unemployed for 24 out of the last 30 weeks. FedNor, another ISTC program, offers grants toward new facilities, expansion, market research or product development for Northern Ontario businesses in manufacturing, processing, business services or aquaculture. Ontario's New Ventures program offers loan guarantees up to $15,000 for new business. Applicants must provide cash equity equal to the loan amount, except in Northern and Eastern Ontario, where the equity requirement is 25 percent. Ontario's Futures program will pay the minimum wage for job trainees. The Ontario Development Corporation offers term loans, loan guarantees and interest subsidies for some businesses in secondary manufacturing. Bear in mind that most government-guaranteed loan programs require the lender to apply the same criteria it applies to its own loans.

That should give readers an idea of some of the programs available. Some have limited funding: they dispose of the monies in their budget, then terminate. Others, such as SBLA, are ongoing programs. Listing them all would occupy several books this size. Suffice it to say that this is an area any new business should investigate when seeking financing. Bear in mind, however, that applying for government assistance can involve you in hours of paperwork, and that the qualifications for many programs are quite specific.

TRADE CREDIT

There are other possibilities as well. We've already seen how Pastic was able to obtain terms from suppliers, enabling him to launch his business without bank financing. Suppliers want to sell product, and will often offer attractive terms to do so. Most want to be paid within 30 days, but as Pastic's experience shows, it's possible to string trade debt out to 90 days. After that, most suppliers will no longer extend credit. Some may apply interest charges on accounts over 30 days.

LEASING

Rather than purchasing assets such as equipment and automobiles, businesses can lease them. Under this arrangement, the lessor owns the asset, and the lessee uses it for a fixed period for a monthly fee. After the period, you can usually buy the equipment for its depreciated value. While car-leasing companies offer very attractive terms, generally it's cheaper to borrow the money and buy other equipment. You should check the implicit interest rate in the lease, and compare it with loan rates. With leasing, your borrowing capacity can often be put to other uses, such as working-capital requirements. The advantages of leasing over purchasing are complex, particularly when taxation factors are considered and are best discussed on a case-by-case basis with your accountant. Leasing companies want to be paid just as much as banks do, and will evaluate your application as vigorously. Because leasing companies charge higher rates, they're usually prepared to take a greater risk than a bank.

FACTORING

For firms with a large number of small accounts, such as wholesalers, using a factoring company may improve cashflow. These services buy your accounts receivable, paying 70 to 90 percent immediately, and the balance on collection. Thus you have to finance only a small part of your accounts receivable. They charge a small percentage of your monthly sales volume. Customers are instructed on your invoices to pay the factoring company, not you. While an expensive source of money, factoring may free you from collection chores and let you focus on other areas of your business.

EQUITY FUNDING

So far we've been discussing debt financing, whereby you or your business incur a debt to obtain capital. In addition, businesses can obtain equity financing, whereby they obtain capital in return for a share in the business.

VENTURE CAPITAL

One form of equity financing is venture capital. For most small businesses, venture capital is not a potential source of financing, particularly startup businesses. But for some high-risk, high-return enterprises, venture capital is a possibility, so let's have a brief look at how it works.

Venture capitalists purchase minority stakes in promising companies, usually 30 to 40 percent. According to a venture-capital rule of thumb, for every 10 startup firms invested in, 2 will succeed, 6 will be marginal and 2 will be write-offs, explains Patrick McGrath, products manager for Venture Economics Canada Limited. (The Toronto-based firm does consulting and research and produces publications for the venture-capital industry.)

Overall, venture capitalists need a return of more than 15 percent per annum on their portfolios. But the high-risk nature of their business means that the successful investments must produce a 40 percent return, McGrath notes. That means that, over seven years, a typical holding period, the firm must show a tenfold increase in value. If a fund manager buys a 30 percent stake in a company for $1 million, for that investment to be successful, the company will have to be worth $25 million to $35 million in seven years. Based on average price-to-earnings ratios of public companies, McGrath believes that for the investment to be successful, the firm must be earning at least $3 million after seven years.

He acknowledges that his analysis is based on "back-of-the-envelope" math, but says it provides a useful test for entrepreneurs looking for venture capital. "Can you look yourself in the mirror and say that in seven years you'll be running a company with earnings greater than $3 million a year?" he asks.

Rather than startups, venture capitalists usually invest in expanding firms. For example, in 1986 Discovery Enterprises Inc. invested $150,000 in Vancouver-based Bedford Software Limited. The investment, small by venture-capital standards ($1 million is a rough average), enabled Bedford to launch its Integrated Accounting program for IBM-compatible microcomputers in the U.S. market. Between fiscal 1986 and 1988, Bedford's sales grew from $750,000 to $5 million, with $8 million forecast for fiscal '89. In a little over two years, the value of Discovery Enterprises' investment tripled.

INVESTMENT CRITERIA

McGrath says venture capitalists evaluate proposals quite different-ly from bankers. They look for inspirational, dynamic managers. "Their focus is not the business or idea, it's the individual who brings them the deal. They'd rather have a Class-A manager with a Class-B idea than vice versa." McGrath tells of one fund manager who applies "the Toledo test: Would you spend a weekend in Toledo with this person?" But fund managers also consider the entrepreneur's experience, and ability to carry through with his or her plans.

Some provincial governments have venture-capital arms that fund new enterprises, especially in high-growth areas such as technology. All private and public venture-capital companies in North America are listed in *Pratt's Guide to Venture Capital Sources*, published by Venture Economics.

Though venture capital isn't a promising source of funding for startup businesses, there are other ways for entrepreneurs to attract investors. Accountants and lawyers are often aware of people looking for investment opportunities. There are also private brokers who match investors and entrepreneurs for a commission. Investors usually want some say in how the company is run. Sometimes they want involvement as a full-time manager, sometimes as a consultant, sometimes as a member of the board. You may be loath to give an outsider a say in how your company's run, but look at it from the investor's point of view. Would you put up money without any say over how the money is used?

MATCHING SERVICES

Matching services are offered by chambers of commerce and the Federal Business Development Bank. For a registration fee of $250, entrepreneurs seeking equity investment can be listed in the FBDB's "Introduction$" publications, which are distributed to people seeking investment opportunities.

Provincial chambers of commerce operate the Canada Opportunities Investment Network (COIN), a computerized database that matches investors and entrepreneurs. The program commenced national operation in early 1989, but has been running in Ontario since 1986. For an annual fee of $250 and $150, respectively, investors and entrepreneurs are listed in the COIN database. Entrepreneurs complete a questionnaire outlining their type of business, amount of capital required, sales facts and projections and current stage of the company. They're also required to file a summary of their business plans. Investors also complete a questionnaire. If the computer finds a "match," COIN sends the entrepreneur's questionnaire to the investor. If the investor is interested, the summary of the business plan is sent; and if interest continues, COIN provides entrepreneur and investor with the other's name and address.

In two years of operation in Ontario, COIN resulted in 364 meetings between investors and entrepreneurs. According to Marge Armstrong, COIN operations manager for the Ontario Chamber of Commerce, this led to about 15 deals totalling $2 million. The majority of these involved individual investors as opposed to venture capitalists.

Hydrobotics Engineering Canada Ltd. of Ajax, Ontario, had developed a marine robotic vehicle, capable of obtaining underwater video pictures, but needed funds to bring the product to market. At the suggestion of his accountant, Clive Thompson registered with COIN in January 1987. He welcomed investor involvement in management, but did not require assistance. Harriet Waterman, the investor, registered in August 1987. Able to provide assistance in marketing, production, finance and management, Waterman sought a position on the board of the target company, as well as the option to work full time or to provide consulting. In December 1987, Waterman's group bought a stake in Hydrobotics for $250,000.

Armstrong says the role sought by investors varies. Some want a seat on the board of directors; others want day-to-day involvement in the company. Some want to take their money out in a few years; others seek a long-term relationship. While the majority of entrepreneurs registered with COIN are startups, most deals involve young companies. She says that's because few startup firms provide enough information on the entrepreneur's background to satisfy investors. Now COIN is soliciting information on entrepreneurs' experience and background to give investors a more complete picture of the investment opportunity. (For more on partnerships and partnership agreements, see Chapter 1.)

There may be unconventional sources of funding for your business. When it comes to raising money, some entrepreneurs can be very creative indeed. Witness Graham Edwards's plan, described in the previous chapter, to sell spaces on his auto-racing board game to corporate sponsors.

Raising money for your company can be a frustrating experience. Russell Knight, associate professor of business administration at the University of Western Ontario, has invited about 750 business owners to his entrepreneurship class in the 15 years he's been teaching the course. "All emerge with a major hatred for banks," he says. "The banks don't want to lend until you're up and running, when you don't need to borrow anymore." Still, any business needs a bank, and most new businesses tend to borrow money. For new businesses banks may be an evil, but they're a necessary evil.

5/LOCATION, LOCATION, LOCATION:
Choosing and Equipping a Business Site

Everyone told Howard Cracower he was crazy to open a computer store on Steeles Ave. W. in suburban Toronto. According to conventional wisdom, businesses buy computers. So for a computer store to succeed, it had to be located near businesses. The first Steals People store was located in an industrial/commercial plaza about 20 miles from Toronto's downtown core.

But Cracower knew what he was doing. Before opening his first store, he had spent 10 months researching his program. Cracower's plan was to apply computer-retailing merchandising concepts that had proven successful in other areas. He travelled all over the United States and Canada, learning from other retailers. "I wanted to see how the winners market," he recalls. "I looked at furniture stores, drug stores, department stores, toy stores, to see what they do to attract and retain customers. I looked at advertising, setup, product selection."

Cracower's research helped him choose his first location. "I wanted an inexpensive warehouse-type location at a major cross street. The location had to be easy to drive to and have lots of parking. Low rent was critical." The first Steals People store qualified on all three counts. True, it's a long way from the downtown core, but it's near highways 400 and 401, two major Toronto expressways. It was inexpensive. And the warehouse-style location helped reinforce The Steals People's image as a low-cost source of computer products.

Cracower's critics questioned whether buyers would travel so far to buy a computer. They believed a high-traffic location, such as a shopping mall or busy downtown street, would be better. But Cracower had noticed the success of other "destination retailers," stores in out-of-the-way low-rent locations that attract customers with low prices or other benefits. Of course, destination retailers have to advertise aggressively to let customers know where they are and what they offer. Besides, a high-traffic mall wouldn't be appropriate for Cracower's operation. Many of the goods The Steals People sells, such as computers and printers, are bulky. Cracower needed a location where people could easily load their purchases into their cars.

In the end, the critics were proven wrong. Cracower opened the first Steals People store on a Thursday in mid-October 1986. By Saturday, almost all the stock had been sold. Sales continued at a rapid clip through December and into the new year. Within three years, The Steals People had grown to six stores, all but one in locations similar to the first.

As we'll see in Chapter 8, location is just one component in a complete marketing plan. The Steals People's success is based on a well-thought-out, well-executed marketing plan, including carefully chosen locations.

LOCATION ISSUES

According to a well-worn real estate proverb, the three most important factors in any real estate deal are location, location and location. That may also be true of businesses selling to the public. For the vast majority of retailers, walk-in or drive-by traffic is the primary source of business. For other kinds of business, location may not directly influence sales. For a manufacturer, access to water, electricity, transportation, labour supply or materials may be the key factors in choosing a location.

Before you shop for a business location, you should sort out your needs and priorities, just as a prudent home-buyer would. How much space do you need immediately, and in the long term? How much rent can you afford? What kind of location do you want: shopping mall, main-street storefront, side-street storefront, office tower, industrial plaza? What special facilities do you need? Do you need parking and access to transportation?

ZONING REGULATIONS
When considering different locations, you should consider zoning bylaws governing the kinds of activities that can be carried out in a given area. While classifications vary from locality to locality, a

common scheme is residential, commercial office, commercial retail, institutional and industrial. These general classifications are broken down farther, adds Ian Cameron, economic development officer for the City of Etobicoke, Ontario. When considering a location, make sure the business activity you plan is allowed under local zoning bylaws.

"Zoning bylaws are there to protect land use," Cameron explains. "Residential areas want to be residential. They don't want intrusions from business. You can have problems in industrial areas with commercial developments moving in. That decreases the tax base of the municipality, since industry is taxed at a higher rate. And industrial jobs pay higher than white-collar jobs, so people spend more in the municipality."

Some businesses won't fall cleanly into any zoning category, Cameron acknowledges. Referring to a large Ontario chain that sells gardening and landscaping products, he asks, "It's not retail; it's not industrial. What is it?" Within most cities' zoning schemes, Cameron notes, there's "lots of room for interpretation."

VARIANCES AND REZONING
If business activities planned for a specific location will conflict with local bylaws, you may be able to obtain a variance, or have the location rezoned. Variances can be obtained quickly, usually within a month. You can apply for a variance if the bylaw violation is minor or technical in nature. But if the planned use is completely different from that stated in the bylaw, you'll have to apply to have the property rezoned to accommodate your use. That requires study by the local planning department and local council. It can take up to a year to process a rezoning application, and there's no guarantee it will be successful, Cameron cautions. If the application is reasonable, it may well succeed. An electrical contractor selling to the public might be allowed to expand from an industrial into an adjoining commercial site. But he says cities often receive applications that are much less reasonable.

MUNICIPAL TAXES
Businesses, like homeowners, pay municipal taxes. They're usually based on the area occupied by the business; and can vary widely from area to area. In Etobicoke, Ontario, for example, taxes are $1.40 per square foot. In adjoining Mississauga, businesses pay 77 cents per square foot. Cameron claims that Etobicoke has better services

such as fire, police, education and transit. "But that's no argument for a guy scratching for life," he acknowledges.

RETAIL LOCATIONS

We've already examined one issue in choosing a retail location. Should you look for a site with established traffic, such as a downtown street or enclosed mall? You'll pay a premium for a premium address. But if the heavy traffic generates continuous sales for your business, your investment will pay dividends. In a mall, you'll benefit by the traffic generated by department stores, supermarkets and specialty chains. In a good street location, you'll benefit by walk-by or drive-by traffic.

However, if you're a specialty retailer, as is Cracower, you may be able to choose a low-rent location. But you'll probably have to advertise heavily to "pull" people to your shop.

KEY QUESTIONS

Retailers of more general products usually depend on walk-by traffic for business. If local traffic is the basis of your trade, look at the quantity and quality of that traffic carefully. Are there enough customers to keep your business going? And are these people your target customers, the kind of people who will buy your product? As mentioned in chapters 2 and 3, you can get demographic information from Statistics Canada or the planning department of your local government. Also look at nearby stores. If their target customers are similar to yours, you'll benefit by the traffic they attract.

TRENDS

When you choose a retail location, you're choosing not just a present but a future. A street location in a declining neighbourhood might work out in the short term, but prove disastrous in the long term. Empty stores, for-lease signs and going-out-of-business sales are signs of trouble. Conversely, a location in a growing neighbourhood might have tremendous long-term potential, even though it looks unpromising initially. For example, there may be new residential or office developments planned for the area that will generate additional traffic. Of course, you have to be able to survive until the potential sales become real.

COMPETITION

Also consider competition. Is there enough traffic to support you and your competitors? If you'll be fighting with a dozen other businesses for the same customers, you may want to contemplate another location. However, it may be better to be where the action is, especially if you offer something your competition does not. In many large cities, furniture, electronics, automobile and other specialty retailers tend to congregate in specific areas. When people are looking for one of these products, they head for the area where sellers of these products are concentrated.

RESTRICTIONS

Look at hours of operation. If they're restricted by municipal bylaw or the landlord, competitors in unrestricted areas may steal your sales while you're forced to close. Conversely, competition in areas where shopping hours are unrestricted may force you to work longer hours than you'd wish. Landlords or municipal bylaws may also restrict the kind of sign you can erect outside your premises.

Finally, consider such basics as transportation and parking. How will people get to your store? Will they have to drive? Is there room for them to park? Will they have to pay for parking? Will they need access to your store to pick up large items? Is that access available? Is the store accessible to public transportation? Will access to your store be inhibited by heavy road traffic?

MANUFACTURING AND DISTRIBUTION LOCATIONS

The parameters that influence a manufacturing location are quite different from those affecting a retail location. Instead of high-visibility high-rent locations, manufacturers and distributors usually require large, low-rent places of business, adequate for current needs and for planned expansion.

TRANSPORTATION

Manufacturers need access to raw materials and to their markets. If raw materials or finished goods have to be shipped long distances, that adds unnecessarily to overhead. To that end, a location with easy access to major transportation corridors is desirable. If your process involves a lot of waste, a location close to your materials source will minimize shipping costs. Conversely, if your products occupy a lot of volume, a location closer to your customers will minimize costs. Close access to raw materials is especially important if you are dealing with perishable items, such as foodstuffs, or if you need continuous supply of materials to keep operating.

LABOUR SUPPLY

You should also consider local labour conditions. As we'll see in Chapter 7, entrepreneurs can't blindly assume they'll be able to hire the staff they need, particularly skilled help. In areas where there is an ample supply of labour, but without the skills you need, you should consider training costs.

MUNICIPAL SERVICES

Before committing to a location, make sure required municipal services are available. Food and beverage processors need access to an abundant water supply, notes Etobicoke planner Cameron. Other manufacturers have large electricity requirements. Before committing to a location, you should determine whether these are available.

If the location lacks specific municipal services but is otherwise favourable, talk to the local planning department, Cameron advises. Any municipality wants to attract and hold an industrial base, and therefore will try to accommodate businesses' needs for electricity, water, sanitation, snow removal and public transit. He tells of one business whose workforce largely comprised recent immigrants. Lacking their own transportation, most depended on public transit. The city arranged transit rerouting to accommodate their needs. In another instance, the city arranged to deepen a large ditch at the bottom of a grade for a business experiencing flooding problems in the spring.

SERVICE LOCATIONS

There are an incredible variety of service businesses. Depending on the type of business, service industries' location needs can vary widely. Service businesses that deal with the public, such as travel agencies, will have location needs similar to those of retailers, particularly if they depend on a steady flow of customers. Other types of service companies, such as car-repair shops, will have needs closer to those of a manufacturer or distributor. They may want a location on a highway, so they'll be visible and accessible. But they'll need adequate work and warehouse space as well.

Service companies whose clients are other businesses will have equally diverse needs. Some might need just office space. An advertising agency might need large areas for storing props or shooting pictures.

In all cases, you should take stock of your needs when looking at locations. You should make it easy for customers to contact your business. And you should be aware of how your location can affect their perception of your company. If they only contact you by phone, you should be able to get by with a less-polished location than if they regularly visit your facility.

AN EXPENSIVE ADDRESS
In some cases, the address itself has a great influence on the way customers perceive your business. "There's no question that location can make or break you," comments Phillip Bliss, executive vice-president of G&S–The Creative Marketing Network, a marketing communications company in Toronto. When Bliss and a partner started The Creative Marketing Network in 1985, they rented inexpensive office space in a northwest Toronto suburb. At $2,000 a month for 1,500 square feet, "it wasn't tacky, but it was eminently affordable," Bliss says. "We didn't have a whole lot of business, so we didn't want a whole lot of risk."

In late 1988, The Creative Marketing Network merged with another agency, which had previously decided to rent expensive space in the heart of downtown Toronto. For 8,000 square feet, the firm now paid $20,000 a month. "The decision happened prior to the merger," Bliss comments. "I'm not certain I'd want that big a cost. But being here has definitely caused a change in the way our company is perceived." The new offices are very close to those of two of Canada's largest advertising agencies. "Till proven otherwise, we're in their league. Big companies will now talk to us."

WORKING FROM YOUR HOME

For many kinds of businesses, working from home is an attractive option. There are many advantages; not least of which is cost.

TRADEOFFS
In addition to saving on rent for business premises, a home-based business lets you write off part of your home expenses for income tax purposes. These include mortgage interest, municipal taxes and utilities. You'll also eliminate the cost and time involved in travelling to and from work every day. You'll enjoy greater flexibility in managing your work and personal lives.

But there are some real disadvantages to working from home as well. You need a lot of discipline to resist distractions–TV, stereo, garden and so on. Other businesses, such as suppliers and customers, may take you less seriously if you're operating from home. Family members, especially young children, may not understand that they can't interrupt you when you're working. Conversely, you may find it hard to get away from your work. Finally, space and facilities available in your home may not be appropriate for your business.

BYLAWS

Some buildings are zoned for multiple uses, such as residential and commercial. In such a case, the owner can operate specified types of business under local bylaws. But if your home is in a residential zone, operating a business from your home will probably contravene local bylaws.

In Etobicoke, for example, technically it's illegal to operate any business in a residential area except for a medical or dental practice. In practice, however, municipal governments are more flexible. "We don't go looking for violations," Cameron explains, "but we do respond to complaints. We don't encourage people to break the law; but we don't want to keep them from making a living either." He tells of his uncle who began handcrafting wooden clocks in his home after he retired. These would later be sold at art shows. "Frankly, I think that's a good use," he comments.

The bottom line is that you can probably do what you want as long as no one complains. It's probably a good idea to check with your neighbours before starting any kind of visible business activity from your home. Certain activities will probably lead to complaints. If you're rebuilding engines in your garage, or if there's a continuous stream of trucks ferrying supplies to your home business, expect a visit from a municipal enforcement officer. A large business sign on your front lawn will probably have the same result. Indeed, one disadvantage of a home business can be lack of visibility.

THE PERSONAL SIDE

In the end, the decision is often personal. Greg Pastic, the record importer we met in the last chapter, has always operated from home. He moved his stock to an outside warehouse in 1984, but still runs the business from a home office. For Pastic, the major advantages were cost savings, a tax write-off on a portion of home expenses, reduced travel time and greater flexibility. "I can get up early, run a computer report, and go back to bed," he comments. Distractions "aren't a temptation," he says. As for the kids, "it's easy to close the door to the office. Besides, it's nice to take a few minutes now and then to talk with my son. He knows not to disturb me when I'm on the phone." He acknowledges that it can be hard to break away from the business. He usually goes back into his office after supper. The only real problem arose when customers would call late at night or on weekends. Now he has an unlisted personal phone number as well as his business line, which he answers only in business hours. "In the beginning I would pick up the phone all the time," he recalls. "But then I realized that most companies keep regular business hours."

After-hours calls were one factor in John Cameron's decision to move his business out of his home. "I had always been surrounded by the business," he recalls. "On Sunday, I'd be taking phone calls from customers." A London, Ontario, window installer whom we'll meet at length in the next chapter, Cameron also wanted to expand his business to include activities not compatible with a home office. Among other things, he wanted to sell glass to the public. After 11 years, he moved to an outside office in early 1988.

LEASES

It's not enough that the location suit your business. If the rent is too high; if you can't get along with the landlord; if your business activities will be unduly restricted; if your competitive position won't be protected, an otherwise favourable location may be totally unacceptable. Not only the location has to be right; the terms under which the location is offered have to be as well.

RENT AND OTHER CHARGES

Rental charges for business properties are usually stated in annual cost per square foot of floor space. A 3,000-square-foot site rented for $10 per square foot will cost $30,000 a year, or $2,500 per month. Depending on the type of lease, you may face other payments as well.

With a net lease, you pay a single monthly fee that covers use of the premises, utilities, maintenance, property tax and so on. The rent may cover all extra costs, or just the extra costs associated with common areas of the building. In the second case, you'll pay your own utility bills. With a net-net lease, you pay a base rent plus a share of all the expenses of operating the building. These include utilities, maintenance, taxes and so on. They may be payable annually after they've been calculated, or the landlord may collect a portion each month. In a retail mall, you may also have to pay a share of promotional expenses. To predict your cash needs, you should be aware of all these charges. You should know when they're due and how they're calculated. Other tenants may be able to give you an idea of the kinds of charges you'll be facing.

A lease may provide for regular rental increases. It may also stagger rental payments unevenly through the year, to accommodate the changing cashflow circumstances of your business.

With retail malls, participating leases are common. Instead of a fixed monthly rent, the landlord takes a percentage of sales or net profit. Tenants may pay a percentage of gross, a base rent plus a percentage of gross, or a percentage of net profit before interest and taxes, to name a few varieties. With a percentage lease, the landlord will probably impose strict reporting requirements on your business to ensure that he or she will receive an appropriate share. There may also be minimum advertising-expenditure requirements. Shopping-centre leases are complex documents and should be reviewed by your accountant and/or lawyer before signing.

TERM AND RENEWAL CONDITIONS

A business lease can last a year, three years, five years, ten years, or any other agreed-upon term. If your location requirements are likely to change soon, a short-term lease may be preferable. However, if the goodwill associated with your business is connected with a specific location, a longer-term lease is desirable. With a short-term lease, you may be forced to move and sacrifice the goodwill you've built up. Similarly, a short-term lease will reduce the value of your business if you want to sell because the goodwill associated with your business will be less secure. If the lease has a clause allowing the landlord to evict you in order to carry out large-scale construction, your position may be as weak as with a short-term lease.

Also consider the conditions for renewing the lease. Are there provisions for automatic renewal? Is there a maximum rent increase that can be applied in a renewed lease?

USE AND COMPETITION

Many leases specify the kinds of business activity you can carry on in that location. Before signing, you should consider the business activities you plan to carry on now, and those you might add in the future. A bookstore, for example, might want to add magazines and stationery at some point. If the lease permitted the tenant to sell only books, expansion options would be restricted.

A non-competition clause will help protect you from other businesses taking your customers. A record store, for example, might seek a clause stating that it will be the only store in the mall (except department stores) permitted to sell records. That would bar the landlord from renting space to other record retailers. In addition, the tenant could invoke the clause if a stereo store in the same mall began selling records.

It's in the tenant's interest to define permitted business activities, and prohibited competition, as broadly as possible. In the case of the former, a broad definition will allow greater flexibility for adding new products and services. In the latter, it will provide maximum protection from competitors.

ASSIGNMENT AND SUBLETTING

At some point, you may decide it's necessary to cut overhead. Subletting part of your business premises may be an attractive option. If your landlord puts use and non-competition clauses in leases, you'll have to confirm that the subtenant's business activities don't conflict with those of other tenants.

If you sell the business, the remaining time on the lease may be an attractive part of the package. An assignment clause will set out the conditions under which the lease can be transferred to a third party. In some cases, subletting or assignment of the lease will not be allowed. In other cases, written permission from the landlord will be required. In others, the landlord will not be permitted to withhold consent without good reason.

DEFAULT PENALTIES

The lease will provide the landlord with recourse should you default. It will spell out the situations that constitute a breach of the lease agreement, such as failure to pay rent, bankruptcy, violation of use clauses, moving out and so on. Should you default on the lease, the landlord may be able to claim accelerated rent for the time remaining on the lease. If you move out two years before the lease is up, the landlord may be able to claim two years' rent. However, the landlord has to attempt to limit his or her damages by renting the space as soon as possible. Even so, with an acceleration clause, you'll be responsible for the landlord's costs plus rent for the time the space was vacant.

Alternatively, there may be a penalty clause limiting your exposure should you breach the lease. A three-month penalty is common. If the space is being leased by a limited company, one or more directors may be required to sign personal guarantees. These may be limited to a specified penalty. Or the guarantors may be made liable for accelerated rent. If you sell the business and assign the lease, be sure to have your personal guarantees removed.

LEASEHOLD IMPROVEMENTS

Under most leases, anything you attach to the walls belongs to the landlord. In some cases, tenants may make expensive improvements that they'll want to take with them when they leave. A manufacturer, for example, might make expensive upgrades to the electrical service. If the manufacturer wished to remove this later, permission would be needed from the landlord unless such permission had been negotiated as part of the lease.

NEGOTIATING

Depending on the property, the terms of the lease may be negotiable. Obviously, there's less room for negotiation with a premier established shopping mall than with a new development with many vacancies.

If the landlord's agent thinks you are committed to his or her location, however, you'll have less negotiating power than if the agent is concerned you'll go elsewhere if the deal isn't right. That will be easier if you develop a list of alternative locations before you begin negotiating. Here the negotiation process isn't unlike buying a house. If the vendor knows you're in love with the property, your bargaining power will be limited.

If you're not a strong negotiator, it may pay to let your lawyer or accountant bargain for you. And you should certainly get their advice before committing to a location. Sometimes, your enthusiasm about a location can get the better of you, causing you to overlook potential problems. Professional advisers can help you look at the location and lease objectively.

LAYOUT AND EQUIPMENT

Once you have a location, you have to get it ready for business. That means laying out the location, decorating it and equipping it. Naturally, the appropriate layout will vary widely from business to business.

Quite often, the first meeting between a business and its customers will take place at the store or office. The place of business can thus create a powerful first impression. Cleanliness, layout, colour, all tell the customer what to expect of your company.

RETAIL LAYOUT

Next to inventory, rent is a retailer's greatest expense; so, it's imperative to use retail floor space as effectively as possible.

The first requirement is an appropriate store decor for your image and target market. The Steals People, for example, wants to convey a discount,"buy now" image. So, Cracower stacks bulky goods in their cartons and displays smaller items on wall shelves. Shopping baskets and carts are arrayed at the entrance. He decorated the store in yellows and reds, his corporate colours."We use the warehouse concept to instill a discount image," he explains."Yellow conveys a discount message, and red conveys urgency." This colour scheme and layout would be totally inappropriate for a seller trying to reach an upscale buyer. There, a sedate, conservative decor, with computers displayed on desks and workstations, would be more appropriate.

USING SPACE EFFECTIVELY

The second requirement is to make optimum use of the prime areas in your store. You can fine-tune layout once you observe traffic patterns in your store. As a rule, people move to the right when they enter a store. Prime retail space includes the right-hand window, the entrance, the right aisle and side of the store. This is where your most profitable and best-selling goods should be displayed. Less-profitable products can be placed in less productive areas, such as rear walls. However, placing frequently purchased items in remote areas may stimulate impulse buying as people traverse the store seeking those items. Supermarkets, for example, know that people almost always buy milk and eggs when they come in the store; so, they place these items in the corner farthest from the entrance, hoping people will pick up other items as they pass through.

There are some general rules for store layout. Products should be grouped logically, so customers can find them easily. Products displayed at eye level and on aisle ends will be purchased more readily. Remember to use lighting appropriately to enhance your products' appearance.

Also consider the possibility of shoplifting. When The Steals People first opened, small products were displayed on tall shelves that provided a perfect hiding place for thieves. Some of these products, such as upscale computer programs, were quite expensive. A few months after opening, Cracower took down the shelves and displayed the goods on the side walls so his staff would have a clear line of sight everywhere in the store.

Manufacturing and Distribution Layout

The requirements for factory and warehouse layout are, of course, vastly different from retail layout. In a factory, the goal is to maximize efficiency and minimize waste. Wasted movement, whether caused by an inefficient assembly-line design or aisles clogged with raw materials, means wasted time. That means higher labour costs. When laying out a factory or warehouse, think about the flow of materials and products through the facility and design it so that the flow is as smooth as possible. The receiving area should be near the storage area for raw materials. The storage area should be close to the beginning of the assembly line. The line should end near the warehouse area for finished product. And that area should be near your shipping area.

Also consider your workforce when designing work space. If the space is well ventilated, well lighted and clean, working conditions will be safer and more pleasant. That will help maximize morale and productivity, and minimize employee absenteeism and turnover.

THE BOTTOM LINE

To get ideas for laying out your place of business, take a page from Cracower's book. He visited a great variety of retailers—not just computer sellers, but all types of merchants. He didn't clone what they were doing, but he learned from them and developed unique and effective store designs for his own operation.

You should do the same. When visiting any business similar to your own, make a mental note of how the location is laid out. If you're particularly brazen, you might even take photographs. By combining ideas from many other businesses with your own ideas, you should be able to develop your own interior plan.

As Bliss has noted, choosing the right location can be a decisive factor in a new business's survival. Excessive rent can have a profoundly negative impact on your bottom line. However, investing in a high-rent location can pay significant dividends.

As Cracower's experience confirms, the right location for one business isn't the right location for every business. If you think about your business needs before searching for a location, you'll improve your chances of finding an appropriate site. And you'll be able to make the most of it once you've located it.

PART II:
MANAGING THE BUSINESS

6/Managing Money
An Introduction to Finance and Administration

John Cameron didn't know what he was in for when he got his first big contract in December 1985. For eight years, he had been doing window and glass installations for residential, commercial and institutional customers in the London, Ontario, area. Operating by himself, out of his home, he was more of a handyman than a businessman.

Then he got a contract to install windows in the new Ontario Psychiatric Hospital in nearby St. Thomas. It took 16 men and 14 months to complete the job. While it promised a good profit, the job created serious cashflow problems for Cameron Window & Glass. "Almost right off the bat, I was in trouble," Cameron recalls. "There were a lot of immediate expenses: wages, overtime, Workers Compensation. Money was going out, but receivables weren't coming in for 45 or 50 days."

Cameron's difficulties became apparent when his bank called to tell him he was over his credit limit. In one case, it refused to honour his payroll cheques. The problem: Cameron's bookkeeping system was in total disarray. "I knew what was happening, but I couldn't get enough control over it to take to the bank. I knew I had spent a bunch of money, and was owed a bunch of money, but that's all."

Cameron realized he needed help. After seeing an advertisement, he contacted the Federal Business Development Bank for its CASE counselling service. The counsellor's first task was to teach Cameron basic bookkeeping, then to detail his business's situation. "It didn't look bad," Cameron remembers. Armed with this information, he was able to talk to his bank and creditors, assuring them that all would be paid. He convinced the bank to honour the bounced payroll cheques, and to keep him in business. "As money came in, things got better."

The counsellor also helped Cameron set goals. Hoping to increase sales, he moved the business from his home to an industrial mall and hired an estimator in February 1988. "After that large contract, I wanted more, and was prepared to do more." The first nine months in the new premises were slow, but a brisk last quarter helped him break even. "We're not out of the hole yet," he comments. "But I've got an accountant and a good line at the bank. I can converse with them in a businesslike manner. I know I have to be disciplined, to get sales up and keep expenses down. If I were starting over again," he adds, "I'd try to be more prepared. I'd have a plan laid out, and I'd have budgets."

KEEPING RECORDS

Cameron's situation isn't uncommon with new businesses. Typically, new businesses are strong on operations or marketing; but are often weak in finance and administration. As Cameron's experience confirms, weak financial management can wreak havoc on a business.

TAX REQUIREMENTS

All businesses have to keep records in order to file tax returns. Individuals have to operate on a calendar-year basis, but businesses and professions can choose any date for their first year-end. A corporation has to file a return within six months of its year-end. Individuals must file by April 30 of the year following the calendar year. After the first year in business, persons and businesses who do not have income tax deducted at the source but expect to pay tax must make quarterly instalments at the end of March, June, September and December. Final income tax payments are due three months after the year-end for Canadian controlled private corporations claiming the small business deduction. Payments for other companies are due two months after year-end. Along with its return, all businesses must submit a statement of income and expenses. Many must also submit a balance sheet. Business records and supporting documents must be kept at your place of business or residence for six years after the return is filed in case Revenue Canada wishes to audit.

STATEMENTS

A statement of income and expenses (or profit and loss statement) begins with the gross sales for the period. Subtracting allowances for returned or damaged goods gives net sales. Subtracting cost of goods sold from net sales gives gross profit. Subtracting operating expenses gives net profit, on which tax is levied. Operating expenses may include payroll (including salaries paid to spouse and children, but only in accordance with their contributions to the business), transportation, rent, utilities, interest, advertising and insurance. Businesses can also deduct depreciation of capital assets such as buildings, cars and equipment. The rate of depreciation varies for different assets. In the first year of ownership, however, you can deduct only half the normally prescribed rate of capital cost allowance for tax purposes.

Your accountant can advise you about the deductions that are allowable, and those that aren't. A general rule of thumb is that any expense incurred in earning income is deductible. But there are a lot of grey areas. Many expenses can be interpreted as either business-related or personal. Some expenses, such as company cars, are regarded as partly business and partly personal. The business portion can be deducted by the company. The personal portion is deemed a taxable benefit to whoever is using the car.

A balance sheet lists the business's assets, liabilities and equity. Assets are listed on the left side of the balance sheet in order of liquidity, that is, the ease with which they can be converted to cash. Current assets – assets expected to turn to cash within a year – are listed first. These include cash on hand, accounts receivable (less allowance for bad debts) and inventory. Fixed assets, items used in the operation of the business and expected to last longer than a year, are listed next. These include land, buildings and equipment, less accumulated depreciation.

Liabilities, money owed by the business, are listed on the right-hand side of the balance sheet. As with assets, current liabilities are listed first. These are debts payable within one year, and include accounts payable, taxes payable and the portion of loans payable within the next year. Next come long-term liabilities, debts not due within the next year. These might include mortgages, bonds and long-term loans. Equity, the value of the business, is also listed on the right-hand side. Equity includes the book value of shares in the business (if it's a corporation) and retained earnings (profits that have been re-invested in the business). Total equity indicates the book value of the business at a given time. Total assets must equal total liabilities and equity; hence the name balance sheet.

ABC MANUFACTURING INC.

Statement of Profit and Loss
for the Year Ending December 31, 1989

Sales		
Gross Sales	$1,000,000.00	
Less: Returns and Allowances	25,000.00	
Equals: Net Sales	975,000.00	975,000.00
Less: Cost of Goods Sold		
Beginning Inventory (finished goods)	100,000.00	
Plus: Purchases	400,000.00	
Plus: Manufacturing Costs	250,000.00	
Equals: Cost of Goods Available for Sale	750,000.00	
Less: Ending Inventory (finished goods)	75,000.00	
Equals: Cost of Goods Sold	675,000.00	675,000.00
Equals: Gross Profit		300,000.00
Less: Operating Expenses		
Advertising and Promotion	20,000.00	
Bad Debts	5,000.00	
Bank Interest and Service Charges	20,000.00	
Depreciation on Equipment	10,000.00	
Insurance	5,000.00	
Local Taxes	5,000.00	
Employees' Wages and Benefits	125,000.00	
Office Supplies	5,000.00	
Owner's Salary	50,000.00	
Repairs and Maintenance	10,000.00	
Telephone and Utilities	5,000.00	
Transportation	10,000.00	
Total Operating Expenses	270,000.00	270,000.00
Equals: Net Operating Profit		30,000.00
Less: Income Tax		10,000.00
Equals: Net Profit After Taxes		$20,000.00

ABC MANUFACTURING INC.

Balance Sheet as of December 31, 1989

Current Assets

Cash and Bank Accounts		35,000.00
Accounts Receivable	151,000.00	
Less Allowance for Bad Debts	1,000.00	150,000.00
Prepaid Expenses		15,000.00
Inventory		175,000.00

Fixed Assets

Land and Buildings	250,000.00	
Less Accumulated Depreciation	25,000.00	225,000.00
Fixtures and Equipment	600,000.00	
Less Accumulated Depreciation	200,000.00	400,000.00
TOTAL ASSETS		1,000,000.00

Current Liabilities

Accounts Payable		200,000.00
Bank Loans		150,000.00
Employee Deductions and Sales Taxes Payable		7,500.00
Income Tax Payable		2,500.00
Current Portion of Long-Term Debt		50,000.00

Long-Term Debt

Mortgages Payable	400,000.00	
Less Current Portion	50,000.00	350,000.00
Loans from Shareholders		40,000.00
Total Liabilities		800,000.00

Shareholders Equity

Share Capital	150,000.00	
Retained Earnings	50,000.00	
Total Shareholders Equity		200,000.00
TOTAL LIABILITIES AND SHAREHOLDERS EQUITY		$1,000,000.00

SALES TAXES

If your business is to sell products, you'll also likely have to collect and remit provincial sales tax unless you live in Alberta, the only province with no sales tax. To do this, you'll have to get a sales-tax licence number from your provincial revenue ministry. You also need this number to be exempt from sales tax on products you buy for resale.

If you're a manufacturer, you may also have to register to pay federal sales tax. The federal sales tax will likely be replaced in 1991 by the new Goods and Services Tax. The new GST will apply to the majority of goods and services produced, imported and consumed in Canada.

Under the GST virtually every business will have to collect tax on all its transactions. The business then remits to the government the difference between the tax it collected and the tax it has paid on purchases. The timing for claiming credits and submitting remittances is just one aspect of the new GST that could have a significant impact on the cash flow of your business. The second book in this series, a tax planning guide for owner/managers, helps to clarify some of the more difficult planning activities the new tax could necessitate.

PAYROLL

Businesses with employees have to withhold income tax, Canada Pension Plan (CPP) and Unemployment Insurance (UI). To do this, you need to get an employee remittance number from Revenue Canada. It takes about a month to process an application. For companies with monthly source deductions under $15,000, monthly remittances for income tax, CPP and UI must be *received* by Revenue Canada the 15th of the following month. Firms with deductions over $15,000 per month must forward deductions twice a month. You'll be charged interest if you're even one day late. Companies also have to withhold the proper amount of tax. That includes tax on taxable benefits, such as the paid health insurance or the personal-use portion of company cars. If a company doesn't withhold the right amount, Revenue Canada may hold it liable if it can't collect from the employee. Employees should pay premiums for such benefits as group drug, dental and disability plans. If the employer pays, employees have to pay income tax on the proceeds when they make claims.

Too often, businesses show up at their accountants a few days before the filing deadline with a shoebox full of receipts. Maybe they'll get their tax returns in on time, but shoebox accounting carries with it serious risks.

EXTERNAL RELATIONS

Good records are also vital for relations with other parties involved in your business. As Cameron found out, without proper financial information it's difficult to talk intelligently to such people as bankers. If your bank is financing your accounts receivable, you must supply monthly aged listings of your receivables. This listing shows debts that are current (under 30 days), between 30 and 60 days old, between 60 and 90 days and over 90 days. If you need additional financing, you have to be able to give lenders and investors a clear picture of the business.

Records are also necessary if you want to sell the business. Poor record-keeping leaves you open to employee fraud, adds Joe Miller, vice-president and Ontario regional general manager for the Federal Business Development Bank of Canada. And without proper records, you may not be able to make insurance claims in the event of a catastrophe, such as a fire. Finally, without good business records, it's impossible to make sound business decisions.

OPTIMIZING CASHFLOW

As Cameron discovered, a business without proper records has no way of knowing who owes it money, how much it's owed and when the money is due; and it has no way of knowing how much money it owes. Without that information, a business can't collect the money it's owed. It has to depend on its customers' willingness to pay on their own. And it can't pay its bills on time.

"Cashflow is the lifeblood of any business," Miller explains. To keep the lifeblood flowing, businesses have to plan, and continuously monitor and update their plans. And they have to pay close attention to the financial end of their operations. "That means managing your sources of financing, your suppliers, your inventory, your accounts receivable," he adds.

ACCOUNTS PAYABLE

Businesses with simple record-keeping needs can use a simple system to manage accounts receivable and payable. When a shipment arrives, the goods should be checked against the packing slip and original purchase order, to make sure you receive the goods you're being charged for. The packing slip should be initialled by the receiver, and put in an alphabetical file of suppliers. When the monthly statements and invoices arrive, they should be checked against packing slips. Inconsistencies between goods shipped and invoiced aren't uncommon. Make sure you don't pay for back-ordered goods. When received, invoices should be filed by due date. To maximize your cashflow, take advantage of the 30-day period most suppliers grant. Some suppliers offer a discount for prompt payment, for example, a 2 percent discount for paying within 10 days. Once an invoice has been paid, it should be stamped "paid" with the cheque number noted, then filed in an alphabetical suppliers' file.

ACCOUNTS RECEIVABLE

Most businesses that sell to other companies offer trade credit. A company with simple needs can use a similar procedure. To maximize cashflow, make sure you send out invoices as soon as possible. Your invoices should advise customers that a monthly interest charge will be applied to overdue accounts. A startup firm might not be able to make that stick with a large important customer, but at least it shows you're serious about collections. Once mailed, invoices should be filed by due date.

Depending on your transaction volume, you might prefer to use ledger cards for customers and suppliers for recording sales and purchases, and managing receivables and payables. A customer card will have the customer's name, contact name, address, phone number and, if appropriate, credit limit, account number and billing date at the top. The body of the card will have columns for recording sales (together with invoice number), payments, dates and running balances.

COLLECTIONS

After 30 to 35 days, customers should be reminded of the outstanding bill by phone or letter. Once they've been reminded a few times, many will pay more quickly. If a customer is consistently late paying bills, you might consider whether it's worthwhile to continue extending credit, especially if you have limited working capital.

Before making a collection call, be sure of your facts. Was the invoice sent on time? Was there an inquiry about the shipment or credit terms? When making the call, make sure you speak with the appropriate person. Be polite, but firm. Ask why the account hasn't been paid, and when it will be paid. There may be good reasons for non-payment, such as personal misfortune, damaged goods or misunderstanding of credit terms. However, the customer may simply have forgotten, may be overextended or may be using trade credit to finance his or her business. You may have to make special arrangements, such as a series of post-dated cheques, to accommodate the customer's circumstances. At the end of the call, thank the party and note the date of the call and payment terms. If they're not met, follow up immediately. If you're unable to collect, your alternatives include having your lawyer attempt to collect the debt, actually suing, or turning the account over to a collection agency, which will charge a commission as high as 50 percent on accounts it collects.

GRANTING CREDIT

Collection problems can be reduced by doing a thorough check on customers requesting credit. Before granting credit, get references from the customer's bank and other suppliers. Ask about the amount owing, amount past due and past performance. Because most businesses try to maintain good relations with their banks, references from suppliers may be more meaningful. You can also turn to reporting agencies such as credit bureaus or Dun & Bradstreet. Depending on the amount of credit requested, you may want to arrange a personal interview and ask for a copy of the customer's financial statements. Besides the customer's history with other suppliers, you might also want to determine the character of the firm's principals, the firm's structure (if it's a partnership or proprietorship, the owners' personal assets can be used to pay creditors) and the principals' skills. With this information, you can decide whether to grant credit, and how much credit to grant. Depending on your situation, you might set the limit as high as the customer asks if his or her past history warrants it; or you might start the customer with a small limit and increase it once a track record is established. You'll want to consider your competitors' practices, your firm's ability to tolerate bad debts and your firm's cashflow needs.

Alternatively, you might choose an amount that is the highest risk you're willing to take. It should be low enough so that a loss, should the customer not pay, won't be devastating to your business. But it should be high enough that most orders fall below the limit. An order below the limit is shipped. Orders above the limit are held till a preliminary credit check is performed. A thorough check should follow as soon as possible. If a customer's order falls below the limit, but it's apparent that future orders will exceed it, begin a credit check.

For some business transactions, it's normal to require some kind of security, such as a lien or mortgage, before granting credit. If the creditor's business fails, then the debtor can seize the security. This is an area where the assistance of a lawyer is essential. For the creditor to be secured, the lien has to be registered under several statutes.

RETAIL CREDIT CARDS

Most firms selling to the public will use bank or member credit cards, such as Visa and American Express, rather than their own charge system. If you want to accept these cards, contact the bank or card issuer to set up an account. The card issuer will charge a commission based on your volume and average sale. However, industry associations such as the Retail Council of Canada have arrangements with card issuers for reduced credit-card commissions to members. Bank card credit vouchers are treated like cash in your daily deposit. Vouchers for member cards are sent to the issuer, and a cheque (less commission) is then sent by return mail.

Before processing a sale, you must obtain authorization from the card issuer, either by telephone or by a credit authorization terminal (CAT) that connects with the issuer's computers. If you're using the phone, you'll be given a floor limit. Any sale above the limit will have to be authorized. If you have a CAT, all sales are usually authorized. This reduces the risk to the card issuer, and speeds up collection, so they usually charge lower commissions to businesses using computerized authorization. If the issuer's authorization procedures are followed, payment is guaranteed.

CHEQUES

Retail businesses also have to set policies for dealing with personal cheques. Should you accept them at all? Should you accept cheques only from known customers? By limiting cheque use, you may also be limiting impulse buying. But too liberal a policy exposes you to fraud.

If you accept cheques, make sure your staff is familiar with verification procedures. Look at the front of the cheque, and verify that the date is correct, that body and figures match, that the amount is the same as that of the sale. Be wary about cheques from out-of-town banks and non-personalized cheques. For identification, many businesses require a driver's licence, plus two other pieces of ID, such as credit cards. It's a good idea to have a rubber stamp made with spaces for name, address, phone, employer, invoice number and identification numbers. The stamp may also contain a declaration for the customer to sign, confirming that there are sufficient funds in his or her bank account to cover the cheque and that funds will remain on deposit.

You can have your bank call the customer's to confirm that funds are on deposit. Alternatively, you can contract with cheque-verification services, which will, for a commission, guarantee cheques as long as you follow their authorization procedures. These usually involve examining the cheque to make sure date and amounts are correct, checking identification and calling the service for authorization.

A cheque may bounce because of insufficient funds, because it was improperly made out (mismatching body and figures, for example), because the account is closed, because it was forged or because the customer stopped payment. If a cheque is returned, contact the customer immediately and determine how he or she intends to rectify the problem. Often, the problem involves a simple oversight, so be polite. Depending on the circumstances and amount, if you're unable to resolve the situation, you can refer the matter to the police, sue in small claims court or turn it over to a collection agency.

YOUR ACCOUNTING SYSTEM

Before you open for business, you should have an accounting system in place. That involves making some basic decisions about the kind of system you want.

COMPUTERIZED ACCOUNTING

First, you have to determine whether you want a manual or computerized system. Until recently, computerized accounting was economically beyond the reach of most small businesses. But since the early 1980s, prices have fallen dramatically. By the end of the decade, the price for entry-level systems was a few thousand dollars.

Basic accounting programs, however, are limited in the number of customers and suppliers they can accommodate, and in the type of management reports they can produce. Larger businesses, or businesses with more complex reporting needs, will need more sophisticated systems. When analysing your computing needs, remember to consider business growth. There's no sense spending time and money installing a system you'll outgrow in a couple of years.

WHAT DO YOU NEED?
Besides the capacity of the system, buyers must also consider needs peculiar to their businesses. Many will find off-the-shelf generic accounting programs adequate. However, you may have specialized needs not met by every package. If you're importing goods, for example, you'll probably need a program that can handle foreign exchange. Other businesses may have more specialized needs. A construction company, for example, has to be able to track materials, manpower and use of machinery in order to bid on jobs and monitor the profitability of projects. Generic accounting programs lack these specialized features. However, specialized programs are available for a wide variety of industries.

A consultant familiar with accounting or an accountant familiar with computers can help you find the right software. He or she will know what issues to address, what questions to ask about your business. Your consultant should be unbiased. If he or she sells specific hardware or software, that's a sign of trouble. Further, find a consultant familiar with your industry, and get references from other businesses he or she has worked for.

ADVANTAGES
Provided it meets the needs of the business, a computerized accounting system has several advantages. First, it reduces the time required for routine bookkeeping chores. With many systems, when you produce an invoice, the customer's account, accounts-receivable summary, sales account and inventory account are all automatically updated. Thus, with one operation, several tasks are accomplished.

After transactions have been entered, computerized accounting systems can automatically produce financial statements. With some programs, you must wait until month-end for statements. With others, you can get an up-to-the-minute view of your business at any time. Either way, you don't have to total transactions yourself to get statements, or wait for your bookkeeper to do it. Some programs let you design your own management reports. Less-flexible programs require you to use pre-designed report forms, which may or may not meet your needs.

Assuming you can get software to meet your needs, your decision should be based on your familiarity with accounting and computers. If you and your staff are not proficient in either area, it's best to take one task at a time. Implement a manual system, then computerize later.

SETTING UP THE SYSTEM

Whether you're implementing a manual or computerized accounting system, the first step is to prepare a *chart of accounts*. Each account will correspond to an income source, expense, asset or liability. Usually, the chart of accounts is developed by your accountant.

It's important that you familiarize your accountant with your business so that he or she can design the system appropriately. Different businesses have different kinds of assets, different cost centres and different income sources. A retailer's major costs are inventory, labour, rent and advertising. A construction firm's are labour, machinery and materials. It's vital that the accounting system be designed properly from the start. Particularly with off-the-shelf computerized accounting system, there's a risk that the system won't fit the business. This unsuitability can have serious consequences. For example, it may make it impossible to track important costs, leading to poor pricing decisions.

DAILY WORK

As the business makes transactions, record them in appropriate accounts. Daily transactions may be recorded in a journal, then "posted" to the appropriate account at week- or month-end. Or they may be entered in accounts as they're made.

Traditional accounting is based on "double-entry" bookkeeping. As the name implies, every transaction results in two entries (or more) into your books. Increases in assets and decreases in liabilities and equity accounts are called "debits"; decreases in assets and increases in liabilities and equity accounts are called "credits." You credit a sales account and debit an expense account. For every debit entry, there must be an equal-value credit entry. If you make a sale to ABC Co., you debit accounts receivable and credit sales. When you receive payment for the sale, you credit accounts receivable and debit your cash account. When you purchase goods, you debit inventory and credit accounts payable. When you pay for them, you debit accounts payable and credit cash. If you need more detail, you might maintain separate accounts for customers, suppliers and different inventory items. At month-end, you'd total these to the main inventory, accounts receivable and payable accounts.

These records are the basis of the financial statements you must file with your tax return: the statement of income and expenses and the balance sheet. Many entrepreneurs leave routine accounting to a controller or bookkeeper so they can concentrate on other aspects of their business, such as marketing and operations. Depending on the needs of the business, that person may work full or part time. Alternatively, they may obtain automated bookkeeping services from their accounting firm. While owner/managers can rely on others to look after day-to-day financial chores and produce statements, they're the ones who have to act on financial information.

MAKING DECISIONS

Complying with the minimum requirements of your bank and Revenue Canada isn't enough to run a business effectively. You need regular financial information to make informed business decisions.

Owner/managers should produce financial statements at least quarterly, and preferably monthly. That way they can react to any situation that affects their business's profitability. Many businesses assume they're making a profit if they're selling product and there's money in the bank.

With regular statements, owner/managers can determine whether or not they're making a profit. From profit-and-loss statements, they can track sales and expenses, comparing them with projections and with previous periods. If sales are down or certain expenses are up, they can determine the reason and take corrective action. This is impossible if managers don't get statements until they file their tax returns.

The balance sheet shows the business's cash and inventory position, how much it's owed by customers, how much it owes to lenders and to suppliers, how much equity it has. This information is vital for important business decisions such as expansion plans, as well as day-to-day management. If your inventory and payables are creeping up, it's important to know as soon as possible so you can take corrective action.

Other businesses may need more specialized reports. Retailers and distributors may want to track sales by product line, customer or salesperson. You can do it manually; but it's much easier with a computer. Once sales transactions have been entered, many programs will produce reports with whatever information you require. If you know which products aren't selling, you can clear them out and purchase products that perform better. If a customer is buying less than last year, it may call for increased sales calls. If you know which products generate the most profit, you can purchase more and promote them more aggressively. You can reward sales people producing the most profit, and motivate those producing the least.

COSTING

In order to set appropriate prices, companies have to build materials and direct labour costs, plus factory overhead and administrative costs, into the price of their product. To calculate labour costs, multiply the time involved in each step by the hourly rate, then add the cost for all the steps. To calculate material costs, you determine the amount of each material needed to produce a single unit, and then multiply the amount by costs.

To these direct costs, you need to add the portion of factory overhead and operating costs that correspond to the product. If a product accounts for half your factory time, you'll probably allocate half your factory overhead to that product. If it accounts for 60 percent of your sales, you'll probably allocate that portion of your general costs to the product. Factory overhead items include employee benefits, repairs and maintenance, factory supplies, utilities, supervisory salaries, rent, insurance and equipment depreciation. Adding the portion of factory overhead that corresponds to the product tells you the manufacturing cost of the product. Adding advertising, sales, transportation, office equipment, owner's and administrative salaries and benefits, interest, legal and accounting, phone and other general office and administrative costs will tell you the total cost of the product as sold.

For other businesses, such as contractors or food processors, costing procedures are similar. If an owner/manager doesn't know his or her costs, pricing decisions boil down to guesswork. In Chapter

11, we'll meet a businessman who got into trouble when he introduced a hot-selling new product. Because he didn't factor all his costs into the price for the product, the more he sold, the more money he lost.

ANALYSIS

Properly analysed, financial statements can provide valuable insights into your own business, a business you're thinking of buying or the business situation of a credit applicant who has supplied statements. You can compare statements with those of previous years, or with your projected performance (see below). You can also learn a lot about the business determining the *ratios* of specific items on the balance sheet and income statement. More important than the ratio at a given time is the trend of a ratio in a business.

LIQUIDITY RATIOS

Liquidity ratios indicate a business's ability to obtain cash. The *current ratio* is calculated by dividing current assets by current liabilities. A business with low current ratio, below 1:1, will probably have trouble meeting its debts in the near future, so may need additional working capital. Inventory can't always be turned to cash as quickly as a business might need. To show whether the business can pay its bills without relying on future sales, the *quick ratio* subtracts inventory from current assets, and divides the difference by current liabilities. A low ratio (below 1:1) shows that the business might soon experience cash problems. A high ratio (say 2:1) might indicate excessive accounts receivable, in which case the business should review its collection practices.

$$\text{Current Ratio} = \frac{\text{Current Assets}}{\text{Current Liabilities}}$$

$$\text{Quick Ratio} = \frac{\text{Current Assets} - \text{Inventory}}{\text{Current Liabilities}}$$

Turnover of receivables is determined by dividing credit sales for a given period by the average accounts receivable during that period (the average of the opening and closing balances). A low ratio indicates collection problems. *Turnover of payables* is determined by dividing purchases by average accounts payable during the period. A low ratio may indicate a poor credit rating. The same information can be gleaned from *average age receivable* and *payable*. If the average age of your receivables is significantly greater than your credit period, your collection procedures probably need review. Average age of receivables is calculated by dividing 365 days by the turnover ratio.

$$\text{Receivables Turnover} = \frac{\text{Credit Sales}}{\text{Average Accounts Receivable}}$$

$$\text{Payables Turnover} = \frac{\text{Purchases}}{\text{Average Accounts Payable}}$$

$$\text{Age of Accounts Receivable} = \frac{\text{Accounts Receivable} \times 365 \text{ Days}}{\text{Sales}}$$

$$\text{Age of Accounts Payable} = \frac{\text{Accounts Payable} \times 365 \text{ Days}}{\text{Purchases}}$$

DEBT RATIOS

Debt-to-equity ratio is calculated by dividing the business's total debt (both current and long-term) by its equity. A high ratio — greater than 1:1 — shows that the business depends heavily on borrowed money, and may not be able to borrow additional funds. A low ratio shows that the business should be able to borrow more if needed. As with other ratios, trends are important. Increasing debt-to-equity ratio shows increasing reliance on debt funding.

$$\text{Debt-to-Equity Ratio} = \frac{\text{Total Liabilities}}{\text{Total Equity}}$$

Inventory turnover is determined by dividing the cost of goods sold over a one-year period by the average inventory for that period. Alternatively, you can divide net sales by the marked-up value of inventory. Low turnover might indicate obsolete inventory, overstocking, poor purchasing or lower-than-expected sales. High turnover might indicate good selection of inventory and effective marketing, or insufficient inventory to meet demand. Dividing 365 by inventory turnover will give the *inventory age* and supply in days. That can help you evaluate your purchasing, and plan future buying.

$$\text{Inventory Turnover} = \frac{\text{Cost of Goods Sold}}{\text{Average Inventory}}$$

$$\text{Inventory Age} = \frac{365 \text{ Days}}{\text{Inventory Turnover}}$$

You can determine *expense ratios* by dividing a specific operating expense by net sales and multiplying by 100. If the ratio is increasing, or if it's greater than average for your industry, you should determine the reason and, if appropriate, take corrective action.

$$\text{Expense Ratio} = \frac{\text{Expense} \times 100}{\text{Net Sales}}$$

PROFITABILITY RATIOS

Gross profit margin is determined by dividing gross profit by net sales. Decreasing margins, or margins less than projected, could be caused by increasing prices for inventory, insufficient markup, theft or spoilage. *Net profit margin* is calculated by dividing net profit after expenses and taxes by total sales. If your gross profit margin is satisfactory but the net margin is not, the culprit is probably excessive operating or general expenses.

$$\text{Gross Profit Margin} = \frac{\text{Gross Profit} \times 100}{\text{Net Sales}}$$

$$\text{Net Profit Margin} = \frac{\text{Net Profit After Taxes} \times 100}{\text{Total Sales}}$$

Return on investment (ROI) shows how wisely a business is using its financial base. It's calculated by dividing the business's after-tax net profit by total assets. ROI below industry norms may indicate a mismanaged business, or simply a cash-rich business that should look at other investment opportunities. ROI above industry average may indicate a well-managed business, but it might also mean the business is undercapitalized. *Return on owners' investment* shows the return the business owners are getting. It's calculated by dividing after-tax profit by owners' equity. If the ratio is low, you have to determine why, and whether it's worth your while to be in this business.

$$\text{Return on Investment} = \frac{\text{Net Profit After Taxes} \times 100}{\text{Total Assets}}$$

$$\text{Return on Owners' Investment} = \frac{\text{Net Profit After Taxes} \times 100}{\text{Owners' Equity}}$$

GROWTH RATIOS

Sales growth is determined by dividing the difference between the current and previous years' sales by the previous year's sales. Similar formulas are used to calculate asset, profit and debt growth. Growth in profit, sales and assets are generally positive signs. Debt growth could result from uncontrolled expenses, or carefully planned expansion. Like all business ratios, these need to be viewed in conjunction with other ratios. If sales have increased dramatically but profits only marginally, there may be problems.

$$\text{Sales Growth} = \frac{\text{Sales This Year} - \text{Sales Last Year} \times 100}{\text{Sales Last Year}}$$

$$\text{Profit Growth} = \frac{\text{Profit This Year} - \text{Profit Last Year} \times 100}{\text{Profit Last Year}}$$

$$\text{Assets Growth} = \frac{\text{Assets This Year} - \text{Assets Last Year} \times 100}{\text{Assets Last Year}}$$

$$\text{Debt Growth} = \frac{\text{Debt This Year} - \text{Debt Last Year} \times 100}{\text{Debt Last Year}}$$

Average ratios vary from industry to industry. Performance judged to be good in one industry might be deemed mediocre in another. Business ratios may be available from your trade association or at the public library. Ratios for a wide variety of industries are published by Statistics Canada and Dun & Bradstreet. Comparing your performance with industry averages will give you a good idea of how you stack up against your competitors.

FINANCIAL PLANNING

Financial statements summarize a business's past performance. But businesses have to be able to look at the future as well, to determine their needs for cash and inventory. And as mentioned in Chapter 3, financial projections are an integral part of your business plan.

PROJECTIONS

Projecting sales is the first step. Some businesses accept orders long in advance, and so can easily predict sales. Existing businesses can base sales projections on previous years, industry trends, economic conditions and related factors. New firms too must watch external trends, but without a history, their predictions may involve as much gut feel as hard fact.

Having predicted sales, the next step is to list all your expenses. Under costing, we've already noted some of the cost components involved in a manufacturing operation. For a manufacturer or similar business to project its profit, it calculates these costs over a year.

Projecting profits is simply a matter of deducting expenses from income. However, to calculate costs, you have to account for inventory at the beginning and end of the year. Adding beginning inventory of raw materials and goods in process to purchases, direct labour and factory overhead, then subtracting ending inventory of raw materials and goods in progress will tell you the cost of goods manufactured. Adding beginning inventory of finished goods to cost of goods manufactured and subtracting ending inventory of finished goods will tell you the cost of goods sold. Subtracting cost of goods sold and operating expenses from sales will give you your profit before taxes.

Beginning Inventory of Raw Materials and Goods in Process + Purchases + Direct Labour + Factory Overhead = Cost of Goods Manufactured

Beginning Inventory of Finished Goods + Cost of Goods Manufactured − Ending Inventory of Finished Goods = Cost of Goods Sold

Sales − Cost of Goods Sold − Operating Expenses = Income

For a non-manufacturing business, income and expense projections are simpler, since they don't have to deal with factory overhead, or inventories of raw materials and goods in process. To calculate income, subtract operating expenses and cost of goods sold from sales.

BREAK-EVEN ANALYSIS

One hopes you're projecting a profit. But as noted in Chapter 3, many companies fail to meet their projections in the first few years of operation. Frequently, sales materialize more slowly than expected, and expenses are higher than expected. So you should determine the minimum sales required to break even.

To do this, you need to isolate *fixed* and *variable costs*. Fixed costs have to be paid regardless of sales. These include rent, interest, equipment depreciation, administrative salaries and telephone. These costs are easy to determine beforehand. Variable costs fluctuate depending on revenue. These include cost of goods sold, advertising, sales commissions, delivery expenses, supplies and maintenance.

To determine your break-even point, first estimate the variable-cost component in each unit sold. Subtracting variable cost per unit from the unit price will tell you the contribution of each unit toward fixed costs. You can then determine the number of units you must sell to meet fixed costs.

$$\text{Contribution Per Unit} = \text{Unit Price} - \text{Variable Cost Per Unit}$$

$$\text{Break-even Point (Unit Sales)} = \frac{\text{Fixed Costs}}{\text{Contribution Per Unit}}$$

Alternatively, you can divide total variable costs by total projected sales in dollars to determine contribution per sales dollar, then divide fixed costs by contribution per sales dollar to determine the dollar volume at which you'll break even.

$$\text{Contribution Per Sales Dollar} = \frac{\text{Variable Costs}}{\text{Sales}}$$

$$\text{Break-even Point (Sales Dollars)} = \frac{\text{Fixed Costs}}{\text{Contribution Per Sales Dollar}}$$

If you're doubtful about your ability to attain the dollar or unit volumes at which you break even, then you should determine which expenses can be reduced in order to improve your break-even scenario. Change the numbers, and repeat the analysis. Lenders will almost certainly ask what will happen if you don't meet your sales projections.

Spreadsheets, a type of computer program, are tailor-made for working out what-if scenarios. You can use a spreadsheet to calculate profit from sales and expenses, or break-even point from expenses. After you've designed a spreadsheet with the appropriate formulas, you enter your projections and the program makes the calculation. It's probably easier to work out a single scenario manually. But the beauty of a spreadsheet is its ability to work out several scenarios. If you want to know what will happen if sales are lower or if expenses are higher than anticipated, change the numbers and the program will show you.

PROJECTING CASHFLOW

Even if you're turning a profit, you may not always have enough cash to cover your expenses. That's exactly what happened with Cameron Window & Glass. Payments for its large contract weren't coming in quickly enough for it to meet expenses such as its expanded payroll.

Cameron's problem isn't unusual. Many retailers run into cashflow problems after the Christmas season. They have no trouble paying September and October bills with November and December sales; but then, in the new year, they have to pay November and December bills with January and February receipts.

New businesses are particularly vulnerable to cashflow crunches. A new store, for example, may have to pay for its stock a month after receiving it. Even if sales are healthy, it will probably take several months for sales to equal the value of inventory on opening day. In addition, there are all the other startup costs faced by any new business, such as fixtures and equipment, and the costs faced by all businesses, such as payroll, rent and insurance. Many otherwise-viable businesses fail just because of short-term cashflow crunches. That's why it is so vital to work out your cash needs in advance.

You should do monthly cashflow projections for your first three years of operation. After determining your cash on hand at the beginning of the month, add receipts for the month: cash sales and collections on accounts receivable. Be realistic when predicting collections: not everyone will pay on time. If you have other sources of cash, for example, the proceeds of a bank loan and the sale of assets, add them to determine total available cash. Then calculate disbursements for the month. These include expenses (payments on accounts payable, salaries, rent, taxes, utilities, insurance, interest, transportation, telephone, travel and so on), loan payments and equity withdrawals. The difference between available cash and disbursements indicates your cash balance for the end of the month. That becomes your opening balance for the next month. If your balance is negative, you have to find additional financing for your business.

You may want to budget funds for replacement of new equipment or capital expenditures. If a machine has a useful life of 10 years, you might include a portion of the replacement cost in each month's cashflow projection. We'll discuss fixed assets in a later chapter.

Creating cashflow projections not only shows your cash needs, it helps you budget expenses. If you face significant cash outlays, you can plan them for months when your cash position is good. If you anticipate a crunch, you can work out a solution in advance.

PLANNING INVENTORY

Inventory is a major expense for many businesses, and, like cashflow, requires careful planning. The purpose of planning is to determine how much inventory to buy, when to buy and what to buy. Because businesses use inventory differently, there are different approaches to planning.

It's not hard to appreciate why inventory decisions are important. If a business has too much money tied up in inventory, it faces higher interest and storage costs. Insufficient inventory may result in lost sales opportunities or an idle production line. If you don't have the right product mix, your inventory dollars are tied up unproductively.

HOW MUCH TO BUY

Many retailers use a method called "open-to-buy" to plan purchases. As the name implies, it shows how much money is available to buy stock. It's easier to do this if you value inventory and purchases in retail dollars, rather than at cost price.

The first step is to project sales month by month. The second step is to decide on the inventory turnover ratio you desire in your business. Published growth rates and turnover ratios for different product categories are available from Statistics Canada, and may be available from your trade association.

You then budget end-of-month inventory levels in retail dollars by multiplying projected sales by desired turnover ratio. Some items will have to be cleared, and others will be stolen or damaged, so estimate markdowns and shrinkage. Add markdowns and shrinkage, and subtract beginning-of-month inventory, and you have budgeted purchases for that month, again in retail dollars. By deducting purchases as they're made, you always know your "open-to-buy" balance. If you buy goods long in advance, deduct their value from the purchase budget in the month when they'll be delivered, rather than the month when the purchase is made.

Budgeted End-of-Month Inventory = Budgeted Sales × Planned Turnover Ratio

Purchase Budget = Budgeted Sales + End-of-Month Inventory + Markdowns + Shrinkage − Beginning-of-Month Inventory

WHAT TO BUY

A retailer's success depends not only on buying the right amount of goods but on buying the goods his or her customers want to buy. You want to avoid merchandise that sits on the shelf; and you want to avoid "stockouts," not having the goods your customers want when they want them. Stockouts result not only in lost sales, but lost customers.

To plan what to buy, you have to consider the various product categories your store carries. Next, determine the percentage of your sales each category represents. With this in mind, you can determine the percentage of your purchase budget to devote to that category.

MONITORING INVENTORY

It's not enough to plan how much inventory to carry, and what goods to buy. You have to monitor your inventory, so that you know when to buy, and when to clear merchandise. Monitoring inventory also helps reduce theft and obsolescence.

Many businesses have seasonal variations. This applies to fashion stores, and to some hard-goods retailers. Sales of snow shovels, for example, are not very brisk in the spring and summer. Stock must be monitored carefully, so that hot-selling goods can be reordered and slow sellers cleared before the end of the season. Keeping goods too long not only increases interest and storage charges, it ties up money that could be invested in goods for the next season. A merchandise calendar can help retailers in seasonal businesses plan their purchases.

Businesses whose product mix fluctuates little from season to season can use a maximum-minimum method for inventory decisions. Maximum and minimum quantities for each item are established. The minimum quantity is influenced by the time it takes suppliers to fill orders. Goods on the list are checked regularly, and when they fall below the minimum, sufficient quantities are ordered to bring them up to the maximum.

Some businesses develop a basic stock list showing all the items they normally carry. A camera store's basic stock list, for example, might include cameras at various price points, lenses, flash units, different kinds of films, batteries, cases, tripods and so on. In addition to goods on the basic stock list, promotional goods might be included in a purchase budget. Whatever method is used to plan inventory, a business must consider projected sales and turnover ratio.

COUNTING THE GOODS

Different businesses use different methods to determine stock on hand. A small business can use "visual control" to determine stock. Essentially, it involves "eyeballing" stock to make sure everything's accounted for. With a "physical count," stock is counted and quantities are recorded. Any business should conduct a physical count at least semi-annually. With "perpetual inventory," a record is kept of incoming and outgoing stock. Movements, and current stock on hand, are noted on inventory cards for each item. Many businesses use a combination of methods.

MANUFACTURERS AND DISTRIBUTORS

For manufacturers, inventory planning works differently. Again, it starts with projecting sales, which is easier, of course, if the company accepts orders long in advance. If it knows how many pieces of each item will be sold in each month, it can determine production plans. It may be more economical to produce units as required, thus keeping inventories of finished goods low. Or it may be more economical to produce them in larger batches, thus minimizing the cost of retooling.

Once it knows when it plans to produce each item, it can calculate monthly raw-materials requirements. Having sufficient quantities of raw materials is vital, since a stockout will necessitate a work stoppage or rescheduling. Stockouts will also affect your ability to deliver on time and, thus, relations with your customers. For this reason, you should allow for supplier lead time when ordering materials, rather than waiting till you have no stock.

Again, ordering decisions will involve weighing costs. It costs time and money to control inventory. A business has to decide which items it makes sense to control. It may exercise tight control over all items. Or only those that represent a large percentage of the dollar value of annual purchases, carrying a long-term supply of those items that represent a small percentage of annual purchases.

On controlled goods, the goal is to balance the costs of ordering goods with the cost of holding them. Ordering costs include preparing purchase orders, expediting (tracking down orders that aren't received on time), receiving, accounting, long-distance calls, stationery and equipment costs. If you're making frequent orders of small quantities of a given item, ordering costs will increase. Holding costs include interest, insurance, warehouse space, increased labour, obsolescence, spoilage and theft. These costs increase when you purchase and store large quantities of a given item. As noted in a Royal Bank publication, *Control of Inventory Investment*, the sum of all costs is minimized when ordering and holding costs are equal. On controlled goods, a business should determine the order size and frequencies at which holding and ordering costs coincide. This method requires perpetual inventory control on controlled items.

THE PAYBACK OF PLANNING

There's a lot of uncertainty in projecting sales, expenses, cashflow and inventory requirements, especially for a new business. But it's a vital exercise, notes Joe Miller of the FBDB. "Individuals have to practise budgeting in their personal lives. It's no different in business, except that there are many more variables. You know your fixed expenses, but not sales and variable expenses. That's why you should be ultra-conservative in year one. Don't mistake potential for what's actually feasible. In the first few months, you may not make a sale. Cashflow has to be planned. You need to create a budget and you need to monitor it once it's made. You should determine reasons for variances, and adjust it continuously."

7/MANAGING PEOPLE:
Hiring, Training and Motivating Employees

For the 1987 tax year, Norma Clement filled out 200 T4 slips, the summaries of wages and deductions employers must give employees at the end of each year so they can file tax returns. Yet the Ambassador Motor Hotel in Sudbury, Ontario, a 20-year-old family business with 2 bars and 45 rooms, employs only 40 people.

Co-owner Clement attributes the high turnover to employee attitudes. "People don't want to work anymore," she complains. "Those that do, work long enough to go on pogey, then quit. You train them, then they up and leave without giving notice."

Clement's problem isn't unusual. Particularly in Southern Ontario, retailers, restaurateurs, contractors, manufacturers and other businesses are experiencing serious difficulty finding and keeping staff. It's less serious in other parts of the country. In Calgary, for example, a three-store ladies' sportswear chain received 500 applications when it advertised job openings in sales in early 1988. During the oil boom, Sunsports/Forzani's would hire people without experience. After the downturn in the oil patch, it could insist on retail experience.

GOOD HELP IS HARD TO FIND ...
Once owner/managers could take an abundant labour supply for granted, but no longer. Experts agree that social safety nets such as unemployment insurance have played a part in the problem. If a job doesn't suit someone, UI is an alternative. Another factor is rising expectations among young people. But there's one overriding factor: demographics.

The retail and hospitality sectors have traditionally relied on young people as their primary labour source. That pool is drying up. In 1981, there were 4,568,695 people between the ages of 15 and 24 in

Canada. They represented 19.2 percent of the population. By 1986, that number had fallen to 4,176,200, 16.5 percent of the total. A look at 1986 census results shows that's just the beginning. There were fewer 15- to 19-year-olds (1,924,855) than 20- to 24-year-olds (2,253,345); and even fewer 10- to 14-year-olds (1,786,600). Then the trend is upward: there were 1,794,975 5- to 10-year-olds; and 1,810,090 children 4 years old or under.

... AND IT'S GETTING HARDER

That means the number of people entering the workforce will decline for the rest of the century. The consequence: shortages of people to fill entry-level positions throughout the 1990s. Ontario is feeling the leading edge of what will become a nation-wide phenomenon, says David Foot, professor of economics at the University of Toronto.

They're already feeling the pinch, says Catherine Swift, chief economist for the Canadian Federation of Independent Business. The CFIB conducts annual surveys in which its 80,000 member companies list their most pressing concerns. For several years, availability of qualified help has been near the top of the list among Ontario and Quebec businesses. Now, Swift says, businesses in high-unemployment areas such as Newfoundland say finding help is a problem.

Businesses that depend on skilled labour, such as contractors and manufacturers, are also experiencing severe labour shortages. And in many industries, the average age of skilled labour is rapidly increasing. With a workforce nearing retirement age, and fewer young people to replace them, the labour crunch in these industries is going to worsen.

The bottom line: don't blindly assume you'll be able to find the people you need. And if you have good employees, do everything possible to keep them.

CONSEQUENCES

One consequence of labour shortages has been to drive wages up. Clement used to pay minimum wage to chambermaids and servers. Now her starting wage for chambermaids is one to two dollars an hour above minimum. Front-desk clerks get even more. "Sometimes they stay, sometimes they don't," Clement says. She says some workers have quit because they were making too much to continue receiving government assistance. She's not willing to scale their hours down, however. "I'd have to train five people to do the work of two," she comments, "and I can't afford that." With room rates in the $40 and $50 range, she can't afford to pay her staff more either, even though that might help.

David Harris, director of communications and member services for the Canadian Restaurant and Food Services Association, says staff shortages have caused some restaurateurs to delay new openings. Others have had to close sections of their restaurants to maintain service levels. Retailers, manufacturers, construction companies and many other types of business are experiencing labour shortages.

EMPLOYERS' ROLE

People aren't as willing to work as they used to be, agrees Dale McNichol, vice-president of the hotel, condominium and restaurant division of Blue Mountain Resorts Ltd. in Collingwood, Ontario. Nonetheless, he believes the hospitality industry has made its labour problems worse. "Many operators have the attitude that there will be another employee in five minutes," he explains. "In the hospitality industry, people aren't treated well in terms of benefits, wages or even understanding the needs of the individual."

Blue Mountain is an exception, McNichol notes. The company has dental, drug, health and pension plans. Employees are given extra days off, for example, birthdays. And they're given more overtime than required by government regulation: triple time at Christmas, for example. Staff are involved in operations through regular meetings and suggestion boxes. They're asked for input on such matters as menu-planning. And they can book ahead for days off.

Wages, benefits and working conditions don't just affect a business's ability to recruit staff. They affect the quality of staff the business can attract. And that affects the image your business presents to the public. "The hospitality industry cries 'whoa' every time the minimum wage is increased," McNichol comments. "Waiters and bartenders are your front-line salespeople. It's ridiculous to think you can pay front-line people minimum."

McNichol's comments can be applied to just about any industry. Whether they're front-line salespeople or back-shop machine operators, employees profoundly affect the quality of your product or service. "Service is what's going to make or break a business in the future," observes Joe Miller, vice-president and Ontario regional general manager for the Federal Business Development Bank of Canada. "Generally, service everywhere is atrocious."

HIRING

The first step to having good employees is to hire effectively, Miller says. He recommends you start by developing a job description. What will the person be doing? What skills will be required?

THE JOB DESCRIPTION

Actually writing a job description forces you to think about the kind of person you're looking for. That makes it simpler to evaluate candidates. It also makes it easier to manage employees once they're hired.

In large corporations, employees usually have specialized functions. In smaller operations, employees usually wear many different hats. That makes it more difficult, but no less necessary, to develop job descriptions. You should lay out all aspects of the employee's function you can think of in the job description, but also note that the employee may be required to perform additional functions. And you should look for someone who's flexible and adaptable, rather than someone who "just wants a job."

The job description should address the skills the employee will need. If you're hiring a mechanic or machine operator, you may have specific experience in mind, and the employee may have to be licensed. You might have to establish a hierarchy of skills, with the most basic skills at the top of the list. For example, it will be desirable for a secretary to know the word-processing program your company uses. But if you want clearly written correspondence, it's more important that a candidate be able to write grammatically and type at a reasonable speed. Word-processing skills can be picked up in a two-day course if necessary.

For some jobs, especially those where the employee is in contact with your customers, personality traits may be more important than basic skills. These should also be addressed in the job description.

McNichol considers an extrovert personality essential for anyone working in the hospitality industry, and looks for this trait in his job candidates. John Asa, general manager of Japan Camera Centre Ltd., a 160-store chain, also considers an outgoing personality essential for retail sales. But knowing how taxing 12-hour days at a retail counter can be, he looks for physical stamina as well.

REMUNERATION

The second step is to set a salary scale, Miller says. To do this, you have to determine wage levels in your area. You can talk to other business owners or to suppliers who know local conditions in your industry. You can also get information on local labour conditions from your Canada Employment and Immigration Commission (CEIC) office.

Besides salary, you should check what other businesses in your industry offer in the way of benefits. If your competitors have employee dental and disability plans or extra paid holidays, you'll probably have to offer them as well. In addition to these tangible benefits, such intangibles as opportunity for advancement and attractive working conditions influence people's job decisions. If you've thought about the type of people who can fill the job you've described and researched other opportunities available to them, you'll have a good idea of what you must offer to attract them.

You may be eligible for training benefits from the federal or provincial government. That information is available at no charge from the FBDB.

RECRUITING

The next step is to make recruitment plans. How do you plan to find employees? By advertising? Through a personnel agency?

If you're advertising for help, your advertisements have to comply with legislation. For example, you're not allowed to specify sex or age in most job advertisements. The local CEIC office can help if you're unsure about the propriety of your ad, says Miller. Your ad should describe the job and the qualifications you've developed. These will include not only skills and experience, but important character traits. The ad should give a salary range and outline employee benefits.

For a fee based on the employee's annual salary, a personnel agency will advertise, screen prospective employees, then refer qualified candidates to you to be interviewed.

No-cost recruitment strategies include placing notices in CEIC offices, placement centres of colleges and universities; taking referrals from current employees or business associates; or simply posting a sign at your business.

SCREENING

If you're accepting applications and résumés by mail, you'll be able to determine the most promising candidates. Besides experience and education, look for continuity in their work history. Are there gaps in their history that indicate periods of unemployment? How long do they usually stay with one employer? Gaps in employment history or frequent job changes don't necessarily mean the candidate is unstable, but they should be addressed in an interview.

The most promising prospects should be invited in for an interview. It's important to put candidates at ease. You should also avoid interruptions, such as phone calls. Miller suggests you interview all candidates on the same day, so that you can make better comparisons. Have a list of questions prepared. You'll learn more if your questions call for long answers, rather than yes-or-no responses. And keep detailed notes, so you don't get confused about applicants once the interviewing is finished.

It's rare that an employer will find exactly the right person, so you should determine which skills and character traits are most important. For a machine operator, mechanical skills may be more important than personality traits or language skills.

Your goal is to determine how closely each candidate matches your job description. You'll want to address the person's work experience, accomplishments and job expectations. You might use some kind of performance test, for such skills as shorthand or typing, as part of your screening process. As well as education, you should determine any extra-curricular activities that may be relevant to the position. Also assess the applicant's personality and presentation.

"I don't look for people who are experienced, I look for people who aren't lazy," says Japan Camera's Asa. "I observe what the applicant does, how he or she walks. I don't ask about cameras, I ask about sports and hobbies. Sports will tell you if the person is a team player, if he or she has endurance. Retail is a wearing occupation. Hobbies will tell you whether someone's an isolationist. Reading and culture are important, but they're not best for retail. Outdoor hobbies are better. They indicate a livelier personality."

Once you've narrowed the field to a few candidates, it's vital to check references. Ask about the candidate's performance, attendance record, personality and honesty. As with the interview, you should be aware of subtle cues that there have been problems with past employers. Advises Miller: "If someone hedges, get nervous. It's what they don't tell you that's important."

ORIENTATION

After candidates have been interviewed and references checked, there may be a clear front-runner, or you may want to interview some applicants again. Once a decision has been made, contact the person you plan to hire to confirm such details as starting dates. You should also inform unsuccessful candidates so they can make other plans.

An employment letter, confirming position, title, salary, benefits and responsibilities should be given to your new employee. New employees should also receive a copy of their job description, so they know what's expected of them. If your firm has a manual of procedures, new employees should receive one when they're hired.

Until someone's actually working for you, you never know for certain how he or she will work out. For that reason, it's customary to have a probationary period before the employee becomes a permanent member of your staff. That gives the employee time to learn the position, and gives you time to evaluate his or her performance. At the end of the period, usually three months, review the new employee's record with him or her. At that time, you can decide whether to hire the person permanently, extend the probationary period or terminate employment. Of course, if it becomes obvious part-way through the probationary period that the person isn't going to work out, it's best to terminate employment right then.

It's important that you make your new staff member feel at home as quickly as possible. The first day, introduce the new person to his or her follow employees and outline their functions. Explain your business to the new employee and indicate where he or she fits in. Make sure the new employee knows who his or her supervisor is, and whom to call in the event of sickness or emergency.

MAXIMIZING PERFORMANCE

A good staff is a critical asset; so if you've hired good employees, it's in your interest to help them perform at their best and to stay with your company. Your goal is to enable your employees to perform their tasks with a minimum of supervision.

TRAINING EMPLOYEES
The first step is to define the skills the employee already has, and those that must be acquired to enable him or her to perform. Depending on the size of your company, you may appoint someone specifically whose duty it is to train new employees. Or, the trainee's supervisor or fellow-employees may do the training. Or you may send the employee to outside training courses.

If yours is a small operation, you'll probably train the employee yourself. To do this, you'll have to think about every aspect of the employee's job. When Sybil Shore started Aloette Cosmetics of Nova Scotia Ltd., a franchised cosmetics home-show selling company, she was the whole firm. "At the beginning I did everything," she recalls, "ship goods, type letters, train managers. I'd pretend I was different people, depending on the task I was doing, knowing some day I'd hire these people. Since I did these things, I was able to train the people I hired."

Once you've determined the skills the employee needs to learn, you teach by explaining the skills—not just what they are, but why they're important—and showing how a task is done. Then step back and let the employee practise, and provide feedback on progress.

Training shouldn't stop once the employee has mastered basic job skills. Successful companies provide training on a continuous basis. Most employees welcome the opportunity to add to their skills. Blue Mountain Resorts sends promising employees to outside courses at universities and colleges. Not only does the company cover the employee's costs, it continues to pay a salary while the employee is on course. The company also brings people in to conduct training, and has a trainer on staff. All this costs a lot of money. On tuition and related expenses alone, the company spends $10,000 to $15,000 a year, not counting employees' wages while on training.

While Blue Mountain's investment in its employees pays dividends, training budgets this high are out of reach for smaller companies. But there are many inexpensive, even free, training options. The Steals People, the office equipment chain we met in Chapter 5, holds meetings for sales and service staff every Saturday morning before store opening. At some meetings, suppliers conduct product training seminars. At others, store managers show staff how to deal with customers.

RETAINING EMPLOYEES

A trained, conscientious employee is a tremendous asset to a business; and a potential asset to other businesses. That has always been true, but with labour shortages affecting some industries, it's especially true now. So you should do everything you can to retain employees.

Employees sometimes leave a company because they can get better jobs with better pay elsewhere. Reviewing employees' compensation packages regularly, and rewarding good performance, will help prevent this. However, if someone else is prepared to pay an employee more than you can afford, there's little you can do. Similarly, employees sometimes leave their firms because they want a career change, or simply because they like to move every few years. Other than wishing the employee all the best, you can't do very much.

But many resignations are preventable. Sometimes employees leave because management doesn't live up to the promises it made when they were hired. Employees often leave because they want a greater challenge, or greater rewards. Even if these problems don't lead to a departure, they cause employees to give less than their best.

MOTIVATING EMPLOYEES

To get the most out of your employees, you have to find out what motivates them.

First, employees have to know what's expected of them. Second, employees have to be given feedback about their performance. They have to know where they stand. Finally, a suitable system of consequences has to be established, so that good performance is rewarded and substandard performance is corrected. All this sounds obvious. But many owner/managers get so caught up in day-to-day tasks that they ignore these management basics.

If you've given your employee a copy of the job description, and if the job description is updated regularly, your employees should know what's expected. Problems occur when people don't know exactly what their jobs are. A sales person, for example, might not know that prospecting for new customers in addition to calling on existing accounts is part of the job.

Feedback should be given often. When employees perform well, congratulate them, and encourage them to maintain their good performance. If there's a problem, don't let it fester. Try to get people to identify their problems themselves, then talk about the consequences for themselves, their fellow-employees and the company.

You should also encourage employees to bring up problems openly and freely. There may be company practices inhibiting them from giving their best. Your management policies should be fair and consistent. Keep expectations and job descriptions reasonable. You're inviting ill feelings if rules are applied differently for different people.

Problems can also occur if your system of rewards and consequences isn't appropriate. Sales people might not make enough calls if they're not given sales targets, for example. Conversely, people are sometimes penalized for good work. A superior typist, for example, might be burdened with extra typing, and become resentful.

The goal is to reward good and discourage substandard performance. For sales people, you might point out the consequences of too few sales calls to corporate sales and their own commissions. You might reward an excellent typist with more responsibility, say training new staff, rather than punishing him or her with extra routine work.

In addition to ongoing feedback and rewards, you should have periodic performance and salary reviews with each employee. At these interviews, you should discuss the employee's work candidly. You should also listen to the employee. Your perception of his or her performance may not be completely accurate, or there may be personal or company problems that detract from performance. In addition to quality, address the person's attendance record and his or her relations with peers and superiors. Outline areas that need improvement and determine whether training is required. Be positive. Cover areas where the person's performance has been good, and determine whether he or she is ready for more responsibility. Based on this information, decide what kind of salary increase is in order. Increases should be a reward for good work, not an automatic right. Performance reviews will be simpler if you maintain a personnel file outlining each employee's work quality, attendance record and other pertinent information.

DISCIPLINING EMPLOYEES

Employee relations don't always go smoothly. Sometimes performance isn't satisfactory; sometimes it slips. Sometimes there are serious problems, such as dishonesty. And sometimes, personalities just clash. It's important to address these problems promptly, rather than letting them fester.

Personnel problems have to be handled resolutely, but also delicately. Poorly handled, they can come back to haunt you in the form of a wrongful-dismissal suit or human-rights complaint. And if you're too fast on the trigger, you might lose an opportunity to turn a problem employee into a valuable one.

Before you fire someone, you should give him or her ample opportunity to correct the problem. And unless the person is being fired for dishonesty or other serious problems, it may be valuable to offer a more generous severance settlement than the law calls for. The goal, says litigation lawyer Jerry Levitan, is to give the employee an opportunity to reform; if you have to dismiss the employee, give him or her an opportunity to minimize damages resulting from the dismissal. We'll discuss unjust dismissal in Chapter 9.

Except in very serious cases, Blue Mountain gives problem employees three chances to reform. The first time a problem arises, the employee's supervisor discusses it with him or her. A written summary of the problem and discussion is entered into the employee's personnel record. If the problem persists, the employee, the supervisor and manager discuss it. Again, the discussion is written up. The employee is asked to sign the summary. The next time the problem occurs, McNichol joins the discussion. Another summary is written, and the employee is given one to five days off to think about the situation. The employee is told that, if the problem occurs again, it probably indicates he or she doesn't fit in. "It's not a threat," McNichol says. "We just tell the employee that maybe this isn't the job he or she wants to be doing."

If possible, McNichol wants to salvage the employee. He says he's fired about 5 people in the last 10 years, "usually for dishonesty. I'm not very forgiving on that. If there's a problem, until we find who's responsible, everyone's integrity is put into question. I have kept people who stole," he adds. "If they're open about it, and offer to make retribution, I'll consider keeping them. There can be occasions when someone doesn't think through the consequences of his or her actions, and is sorry afterward. But if someone lies about it when confronted, I lose respect for that person."

Not all employers are as generous as McNichol in handling problems. But they should follow his scheme. Discussing the problem with the employee can lead to eliminating the problem and salvaging the employee.

LEGAL REQUIREMENTS

Having employees exposes you to several legal obligations. You'll have to deduct income tax, Unemployment Insurance (UI) premiums and Canada Pension Plan (CPP) contributions from employees' paycheques, and make your own contributions. The employer's share of CPP contributions is equal to the employee's; for UI, the employer's share is 1.4 times the employee's. Withholding tax, CPP and UI have to be remitted each month to Revenue Canada. To do this, you need an Employer's Kit, which includes employer's guides, deduction tables, T4 slips, remittance forms and employee exemption forms.

You're also required to maintain payroll records. These should include wage rate, hours worked, gross wages and deductions. In addition to updating the record for each pay period, you'll have to provide monthly summaries with your remittances to Revenue Canada and annual summaries on the T4 slips you give employees. When a person's employment with you ends, you must send a Record of Employment to your local CEIC office.

Each province requires employers to adhere to standards in their relations with employees. These standards include minimum wages, annual vacations, statutory holidays, hours of work, days off, overtime, dismissal and severance pay. Your workplace may also be governed by health and safety regulations. Publications outlining employers' obligations are issued by provincial ministries of labour. Depending on your industry, you may also be required to make contributions to the Worker's Compensation Board.

All businesses are governed by federal or provincial human-rights codes that forbid discrimination in hiring, promotion and disciplinary practices on the basis of race, nationality, religion, political beliefs, sex, age, marital status and some other areas. If a complaint is upheld, you may be required to pay a fine and/or damages to the employee, as well as re-instating him or her. Because of the way human-rights codes are administered, it's not sufficient to refrain from discrimination, says Levitan. You should avoid any conduct, such as racial jokes, that could be considered discriminatory.

"ENTREPRENEUR, MANAGE THYSELF"

The major attraction of having your own business is being your own boss. But to succeed, you have to be just that—your own boss. Managing your staff effectively is a big part of running a successful business, but you also have to manage yourself effectively.

In any day, there will always be more tasks to accomplish than there are minutes, so you have to organize your time. Make "to-do" lists of things you want to accomplish. Arrange tasks in order of priority: vital, valuable and unimportant. Be willing to say no to requests you don't have time for. You'll have enough important things to do without spending time on unimportant ones.

Determine which tasks you can delegate, then do it. There's no sense paying employees if you don't make the most of them. It may take more time to train someone to handle a task than it takes you to do it yourself. But from then on, the employee can perform it, freeing you for tasks you can't delegate. Insist that staff do work properly, rather than fixing it for them. Again, that might take more time, but it will pay dividends later.

Maintain a diary of meetings you have to attend and phone calls you have to make. Try to stick to the schedule you set. Start and end meetings on time. Prepare for meetings and phone calls before starting. Have the documents you need ready at hand. Get down to business right away, rather than chatting about the weather or last night's hockey game.

Before embarking on long-term projects, establish milestones for completing key parts of the project. Usually the hardest part of any project is starting. So don't procrastinate.

If you organize files, you won't waste time looking for needed information. Before you file something, decide whether you really will need it in the future.

Try to eliminate time-wasting activities, such as reading brochures and junk mail. Learn to dispose of unwanted visitors or callers quickly.

More than almost any factor, the way you manage yourself and your employees will determine the success of your venture. Remarks Russell Knight, associate professor of entrepreneurship at the University of Western Ontario's school of business administration: "The people side of a business is very important; it can make or break a business. Many entrepreneurs are independent types, and tend to give this short shrift."

8 / DEALING WITH CUSTOMERS:
An Introduction to Marketing and Sales

Alistair Davidson and Mary Chung faced a huge challenge when they took their new personal-computer software package to market in 1985. Their company, Toronto-based Alacritous Inc., had developed a program to help businesses develop and fine-tune their financial and marketing strategies. It was the first program to offer this function, and it was based on leading-edge technology not previously used on personal computers. Developing the product had been challenge enough. Now they had to get the message to potential customers. Their success shows they did a lot of things right. But one flaw in their plan had a significant cost.

Davidson and Chung were marketing professionals before they started their computer software company in 1985. Chung had worked in consumer-goods marketing, advertising and sales for several organizations after obtaining an MBA from UCLA. A Harvard MBA graduate, Davidson has worked as a business strategy consultant for Woods Gordon and Laventhol & Horwath.

While teaching a course on business strategy at Toronto's York University in 1984, they noticed that errors commonly made by businesses were also being made by students. "People have a hard time asking the right questions about their business," Davidson remarks. These questions include, "On what basis am I trying to compete?" "Who are the principal stakeholders (such as suppliers and customers) who can affect my success?"

While driving home after a lecture in January 1985, Davidson and Chung asked themselves, "Wouldn't it be nice if there were some software that would help people ask the right questions?" An idea was born. By June, Alacritous had a rough prototype. Chung and Davidson showed it to 200 people, including bankers, planners and senior executives responsible for finance. Based on this "concept test," they decided to proceed.

Alacrity, their first product, belongs to a class of computer programs called "expert systems." These programs contain the knowledge of one or more experts in a given field. Medical expert systems are available to help physicians diagnose disease. There are expert systems to help engineers design electronic circuits and to help geologists with mine exploration.

Alacrity was based on Davidson's and Chung's course knowledge and experience. The program "interviews" the user just as a marketing consultant would, asking approximately 100 questions about the business, such as, "What stage of development has this served market reached?" "What are the overall difficulties for new entrants entering this market?" "How do you rate this business's financial risks?" "Does this business compete in the broad segment of the market rather than in a narrow niche?"

Then, based on the users' responses and 3,000 business rules of thumb in its "knowledge base," Alacrity creates a 25-page report using pre-written paragraphs. Areas covered include economic conditions in relation to the business, the business's competitive strengths, growth of the business versus the market, stability of the market, market barriers and structure, advertising and promotion, pricing and value issues, planning issues, probable competitive risks and competitive moves.

MARKETING THE PRODUCT

Alacrity was a brand-new product using brand-new technology in a brand-new industry. All previous expert systems were targeted at specialized fields; most ran on large, expensive computers. Alacrity was aimed at a mass business audience and ran on relatively inexpensive personal computers. At $4,500, it was expensive compared to most PC programs, but cheap for an expert system. How could a new firm with limited funding get this message across to a large audience?

SEVERAL SMART DECISIONS ...
Davidson and Chung made some smart decisions. Earlier, their firm had formed a strategic alliance with Ashton Tate, a giant California software company. The initial version of Alacrity worked in conjunction with an Ashton Tate program called "Framework."

Framework has its own word-processing, spreadsheet, database, graphics and communications functions, so these didn't have to be built into Alacrity. In addition to providing technical assistance, the alliance enabled Alacritous Inc. to piggyback onto Ashton Tate's marketing and distribution network. Ashton Tate distributed demonstration programs of Alacrity to its dealers and involved Alacritous in its sales seminars.

To minimize sales costs, they set up a direct-sales force to market to large organizations that would buy multiple copies of their program. That meant they had to forgo individual sales to small companies. But it let them make the most of limited sales and marketing resources.

To compensate for a limited advertising budget, the firm worked hard to obtain press coverage. In addition to several computer-industry publications, it was covered in general business magazines such as *Canadian Business.*

... AND ONE SLIP

However, Davidson and Chung had become so caught up in their product's technology that they initially lost sight of its benefits. Their literature trumpeted Alacrity as a product that would let you do a strategic analysis of your business in a few minutes. But it didn't explains the benefits of the analysis.

They slowly realized their mistake as they watched customers during sales seminars. When different groups from the same company tried Alacrity, using information about their business, there would be heated—but productive—discussions about the strategic assumptions behind the clients' business. Almost inevitably, they'd end up buying the product. As Davidson and Chung saw this happening, it dawned on them that users didn't care about the glamorous technology behind Alacrity; they cared about what it accomplished in their businesses. After Alacrity had been on the market for a year, they began stressing these benefits in their promotional material and sales presentations. The result: the rate of closings at sales presentations increased between two and four times.

THE LESSON

Davidson is philosophical about this part of his firm's history, calling it part of a learning curve all companies go through. "In fact, we feel we learned more quickly than most companies would have," he comments. While costly, these misplaced marketing efforts didn't do lasting damage to Alacritous. By early 1989, its programs were enjoying brisk sales in Canada, the United States and Europe. Still, Davidson says had they stressed Alacrity's benefits from the outset, Alacritous would have reached this point a year earlier. He estimates the lost time cost the company between a quarter and half of its equity capital. "The irony is that Mary and I are not technology people," he comments. "We're marketers. But this kind of thing happens consistently. If you understand a complex product, there's a huge gulf between you and the people to whom you're trying to market it. The marketing challenge is to communicate the product's benefits in a simple fashion to someone who doesn't understand it."

Alacritous Inc.'s experience shows how important marketing decisions are. Making a simple adjustment to an otherwise sound marketing program paid huge dividends for Alacritous. It also shows how complicated marketing decisions are. If seasoned marketers such as Davidson and Chung, selling a product closely concerned with marketing, make a slip on their marketing learning curve, that curve must be pretty steep.

MARKETING BASICS

Marketing and production are the two essential elements of any business—large or small—says Ron Rotenberg, associate professor of marketing and management at Brock University in St. Catharines, Ontario. Mark Twain's famous observation, "If you build a better mousetrap, the world will beat a path to your door," probably wasn't true in the nineteenth century. It's certainly not true today. Elaborates Rotenberg: "To stay in business, you need a good product or service, and you need to market it. You can't expect the market to come to you."

Rotenberg says many businesses, especially small businesses, equate selling with marketing. In fact, it's a much broader activity. "Sales are part of marketing, but marketing goes beyond selling." It encompasses every aspect of getting your product into customers' hands. To market your product successfully, you have to balance a whole slew of interrelated factors: the product itself, distribution channels, place of business, pricing strategies, advertising and, of course, selling. Your plans have to take into account your target customers, and external factors such as economic conditions.

"What's My Line?"

Before you can develop marketing plans, you have to do some preparatory work. First of all, you have to define what business you're in. That might seem obvious, but, as Davidson notes, it's a task undertaken by too few businesses. What product are you selling? What does it do for buyers? As Alacritous's experience shows, you should define your benefits clearly. Its sales took off when it defined its product as a business-planning system rather than as a slick piece of software. As we'll see, this realization had a significant impact on Alacritous's marketing strategy.

You also have to define the nature of your business. Are you a manufacturer, a distributor, a retailer? Again, this seems obvious. But businesses get into trouble because their activities conflict. In addition to selling its line of personal computers to retail stores, a Toronto manufacturer sold direct to end-users, undercutting its own dealers in the process. When its largest account discovered this, it dropped the line like a hot potato.

Finally, you have to set goals. How large a player do you want to be? What portion of the market do you expect to gain? If you're a retailer, do you want to operate a single store, or do you expect to grow into a national chain? Your goals will have a profound impact on your marketing strategies. It will be the basis of vital decisions such as inventory levels, location and advertising. If you start with out clear goals, your marketing efforts will be poorly focused.

Who Are My Customers?

As well as defining your business, you have to identify your customers. As noted in Chapter 2, your customer profile might be a natural corollary of your business type. Then again, you might have to select a portion of the total market to pursue. You may define your market by age, sex, income, education, marital status, religion, home ownership, ethnicity, occupation, geographical location or a host of other criteria. The purpose is to have a market large enough to provide you with a growing business, but focused enough to enable you to market effectively.

If you're opening a clothing store, are you going to sell to children or adults? To men or women? To young, middle-aged or older customers? To budget-minded, middle-class or affluent buyers? It takes a giant such as Dylex or the Grafton Group to address all areas of the clothing market, and they use different store identities to do it. A common mistake is to try to do many things, to be all things to all people. The result is diffuse marketing efforts that never make a real impact in any of the markets.

POSITIONING

The next step is to distinguish yourself from your competitors. Through advertising and other means, you position yourself as better than or different from other companies in your market. Alternatively, you might select an underserved part of the market, where competition is lower.

That's the strategy used by Magnum Dynalab Ltd., the stereo-equipment manufacturer we met in Chapter 1. The company got into trouble when giant offshore manufacturers invaded the Canadian market in the mid-1970s. Magnum was producing mid-price AM/FM receivers for the mass market. Manfred Breunig, then the sole owner and now a partner, insists his products were as good as those of his Japanese competitors, but their massive marketing resources made it impossible for him to compete. Eventually, he had to stop producing the receivers. He hung on for a decade, producing specialized audio accessories. Then, in 1984, he built an upmarket FM tuner sure to appeal to audio enthusiasts. The tuner lacked convenience features found on Japanese models, but it contained circuitry designed to enhance sound quality. Rather than the mass market, it appealed to a smaller market of audiophiles, many of whom have a distaste for equipment from mass-market producers. There were U.S., British and Canadian companies building high-end audio components such as amplifiers and loudspeakers, but no one was concentrating on high-end tuners. The company now has a solid North American base of dealers, and exports to Europe and Asia. The product fit into a market niche large enough to support Magnum Dynalab and provide room for growth, yet secure from large competitors.

THE "FOUR Ps"

Few small companies consciously define their businesses or identify their customers, says Derek Lackey, president of Lackey Advertising Inc., an Oakville, Ontario, advertising agency. Lackey, who worked in advertising sales and design for 12 years before forming his own agency, says most small businesses know the answers to these questions, but never bother to ask them. Having these answers is critical if you want to make intelligent marketing decisions. A complete marketing strategy consists of something marketers call "the four Ps."

THE PRODUCT

Product includes more than just your goods or services. It includes such things as packaging, presentation, warranty and service. Businesses have to study their market to determine what their product should be like. Is your product compatible with the image you're trying to establish? Does it appeal to your customers? Retailers, for example, will want to carry a product mix that will appeal to their target market.

Toronto-based Japan Camera Centre Ltd. has 160 franchised and corporate outlets, mostly located in shopping centres. Its customers are drawn by convenient mall locations and its one-hour photo-finishing service. "Our customers aren't professional photographers or advanced amateurs," explains general manager John Asa. "So we select merchandise that best meets their needs: easy-to-use point-and-shoot cameras ranging from $50 to $500. We'll lose the customers who want very sophisticated cameras, but we don't mind that. We can't be everything to everyone." This disciplined approach is vital to Japan Camera's success, he adds.

For a manufacturer, it might seem like putting the cart before the horse to examine the market, then design a product for it. But that's what successful companies do. They look at their customers' needs, then build products to meet those needs. It's not a one-shot process: successful marketing involves dialogue between the supplier and customer. The seller informs the buyer about the product; but the seller should also take care to determine the buyer's needs.

That's what Alacritous did. When it released new versions of its programs, it incorporated features customers had asked for, such as the ability to go backwards and change one's mind about a question. They made the program easier to use. They introduced additional programs with new functions requested by customers. "We listened to everything our customers had to say about the product," Davidson notes.

Listening to the market often makes the difference between a marginal product and a very successful one, Rotenberg says. And often, offering what the customer wants can involve only a minor adjustment in the product.

THE PLACE

The second of the four Ps is *place*. The term is used very loosely in this context and refers to the measures the business takes to get product into the customers' hands. Only in the context of retailing can the term be taken literally, since a retailer's place of business is the means by which products are put into customers' hands. Just because a retail location is busy doesn't mean it's appropriate for every retailer. As with other marketing decisions, "place" decisions should be based on the type of business, profile and target market.

Rather than locations with the richest customer base, John Asa of Japan Camera says his company looks for locations with a customer base that corresponds to its middle-of-the-road market. "We want the mall's customers to be our customers," he explains.

For this, he relies on demographic information supplied by the landlord, plus gut feel. He's aware that demographic information may be several years out of date. For example, Japan Camera agreed in 1973 to lease a store in the Square One Mall in Mississauga, Ontario, before it was built. "At that time, the population of the area was sparse," Asa recalls. "But Toronto was growing and had to spread out." Located at the intersection of two major highways, Square One had excellent possibilities, even though the statistics didn't show it.

For other kinds of businesses, "place" involves every aspect of packaging and movement of product. It involves decisions about distribution channels. A manufacturer, for example, has to decide whether to sell directly to customers or to use retailers and distributors. If selling through outside distributors and/or retailers, the manufacturer must make it more attractive for them to sell his or her, rather than competitors', product. Decisions must be made about warehousing locations and shipping methods. When Alacritous decided to use a direct-sales force rather than distributors and retailers, it was making a "place" decision.

THE PRICE

The third P is *price*. Many small businesses make pricing decisions on a "cost-plus" basis, Rotenberg notes. To determine the selling price of their product, they total their costs and add desired profit. While costing issues must inform any pricing decision, in the end it's a marketing issue rather than an accounting one, he believes. Customers may be willing to pay a higher price, so the business may be forgoing profits. In some areas, such as perfume or liquor, a higher price many actually increase sales. A business may choose not to compete on price, but instead offer a product with premium benefits.

Aside from your costs, your pricing may be influenced by competition. Depending on your goals, you might try to set the same prices as your competitors. You might try to entice buyers with lower prices. Or you might set higher prices based on service, image, location, product quality or other factors. You should also consider your product's lifecycle. If it's short, you'll have less time to recoup your development costs; and your pricing should reflect this.

Alacritous's Davidson lists some other issues that should inform pricing policy: the company's strategic goals, its target market, its capacity, and the value relative to other similar products. "If you're running at capacity, you can raise prices as a way of controlling demand," he notes. A firm may launch its product at an attractive price, as Davidson did, to get a toehold in the market, then raise prices once it's established. It might hold prices down to keep competitors out, or it might elevate them slightly if it can count on customer loyalty. If it's selling a scarce product, it might price the product very high (risking sour customer relations in the process). If it needs money and has excess inventory, it might lower prices temporarily.

It's not uncommon to have several pricing policies at once. Retailers sometimes offer low-priced product as loss-leaders to attract customers, hoping they'll also buy regular-priced products.

Your pricing strategy will do a lot to define your position in the market. Selling low-quality goods at a low price will identify you as a cheap supplier; high-quality goods at a high price positions you as a premium supplier. Mid-range goods at an average price puts you in the middle as a fair-value supplier. Of course, it's possible to pursue other product-pricing strategies. If you don't plan to be around very long, you might decide to fleece the market by selling cheap goods at a high price. You might sell quality goods at a medium or low price to grab a chunk of the market. Regardless of your strategy, remember that your initial moves will say a lot about your company; and that a reputation, once established, is very hard to change.

PROMOTION

All methods of communicating with potential customers are included in *promotion*—"any technique aimed at facilitating sales of goods or services," to use Rotenberg's words. Businesses have a bewildering array of promotional possibilities. These include print advertising in newspapers and magazines and in the Yellow Pages, radio and TV advertising, signs, ads on buses and in transit shelters. Aside from advertising, entrepreneurs can promote their businesses by direct mail, through tradeshow exhibits, with coupons, contests, special events, window displays, point-of-purchase displays, publicity. Personal selling and packaging are also key components in most companies' promotion strategies.

Each has its advantages. Newspapers reach large audiences, but specialized groups can be targeted by choosing specific sections, such as the sports or business pages. They're timely, so advertising can be co-ordinated with specific events. Ethnic or community newspapers can help you reach narrowly targeted groups at a reasonable cost, but may not reach all your customers. The higher circulation a newspaper has, the higher its rates will be. You'll pay a premium if you want special position; and volume discounts will be offered based on the space you buy over a one-year period. Specialized magazines also let you reach narrowly targeted readers. Radio advertising enables you to reach specific audiences by choosing stations. Frequent repetition is needed for radio advertising to bear fruit, and times for radio "spots" need to be carefully chosen. Television can be effective, but production and time costs can be prohibitive for smaller businesses. With radio and TV, charges are higher for periods with greatest viewership or listenership: prime time (7:00 to 11:00 p.m.) for TV and drive time (morning and afternoon rush hours) for radio. Charges are also based on audience size: the greater the station's audience, the higher the rates.

With direct mail, you can send your message to exactly the people you want to receive it. In addition to using your own customer lists, you can obtain mailing lists from direct-mail companies, trade associations and directories. If you're buying someone else's list, Lackey suggests you deal with a firm that has to keep its records up to date, such as a credit-card company. That way, the list is more likely to be accurate.

If you're a manufacturer or distributor, you might set part of your promotional budget aside for your dealers. This co-operative advertising fund subsidizes local advertising of your product. By helping your dealers sell, you increase your own sales.

Just about any firm will use several promotional vehicles. A store might place coupons or promote special events in its newspaper advertising and direct mail.

ADVERTISING STRATEGY

For your advertising to be effective, you need a strategy. You have to know how much you're going to advertise, what you're going to advertise, when you're going to advertise, where you're going to advertise, how you're going to advertise and why you're going to advertise.

PLANNING

Before you can formulate a strategy, you have to know what your objectives are. Are you a new business trying to establish an identity? If so, you'll probably have to devote more money to advertising than an existing business with an established identity would. Do you want to promote specific products, or build awareness of your business? Are you trying to steal customers from your competitors or attract customers your competition hasn't reached?

You should also have an objective for each individual ad. Are you trying to build awareness of a product or get customers into a store to buy it? The objective might be sales of advertised items, phone calls to a toll-free number or increased store traffic. By formulating specific objectives, you can evaluate the success of your advertisement.

BUDGETS

Once you know your goals, you're in a good position to establish an advertising budget. That budget might be influenced by what your competitors are doing. If they advertise heavily, you may have to do the same. However, you might have an edge such as a more convenient location that reduces the need for competitive advertising.

You might base your budget on sales, or if you're a new business, projected sales. The most appropriate proportion to allot to advertising will vary from business to business. Your trade association should be able to advise you of what the average is for your industry. In some cases, such as an industrial manufacturer selling to a few key accounts, it may be minimal. In other cases, such as retailers in very competitive fields, it can be close to 10 percent.

Budgeting decisions will also be influenced by your business's financial resources, including co-op assistance from suppliers.

TIMING

To get the most for your promotional dollar, you have to advertise at appropriate times. Rather than purchasing ads whenever a media rep calls, you should co-ordinate advertising with times of highest demand for your product. For a retailer of children's clothing, this might be August, just before kids go back to school. For a toy store, it might be November and December, just before Christmas. Manufacturers and distributors supplying these stores might do consumer advertising at the same time, but also run trade promotions several months earlier, when retailers are making buying decisions. As well as when to advertise, you should plan what you're going to advertise, promoting different items when their demand is highest. You also have to decide how frequently you're going to advertise. If you're trying to establish awareness for your business, a couple of ads won't be enough. An advertising calendar helps you plan your ads in advance.

MEDIA CHOICE

When choosing media, your object is to reach as many of your target customers as possible, for the lowest possible cost. The key questions are: "Are their readers (or listeners or viewers) my customers? What does it cost to reach them?" You should try to use media that reach as many of your customers as possible, but avoid paying to reach people who aren't your customers. Media sales representatives can supply demographic data on their audiences. You can supplement that information by calling their advertisers and asking how effective the medium is.

A company selling a consumer product may well benefit by consumer advertising, perhaps in newspapers and radio. Widely used business products such as computers and FAX machines are regularly advertised in mass media by manufacturers and retailers, especially in the business pages. But sellers of specialized industrial products might get more bang for their promotional dollars by personal selling, supplemented by ads in trade magazines and participation in tradeshows.

The chosen vehicle should help you realize your long-term and specific advertising goals. You might use the same media as your competition does, or you might select different media to try and reach different customers.

THE MESSAGE

Your advertising message should reflect your customers' needs and your company's personality, and promote your long-term and specific advertising goals. You should make it a point of knowing why customers patronize your business, and appeal to those reasons.

In other words, you should sell your strengths. A budget clothing store will probably stress price; an upscale retailer will emphasize produce quality and service. Illustrations will help get your message across, but they should be accurate.

Whatever the message, it should be simple. Too many ideas in an ad reduce its impact. Use language your customers can understand. Ads should emphasize benefits for your customers, not just product features. It should contain essential information, such as the company's address and phone number, so customers know where they can buy your product.

Finally, make sure everything about your ad is accurate and in good taste. Most media have guidelines about what kinds of advertising are acceptable. In addition, advertising and sales are covered by various federal and provincial laws. It's illegal to misrepresent your goods (as new, when they're used, for example, or as premium quality when they're not); to misrepresent your pricing (advertising an every-day price as a "sale" price, or using "bait-and-switch" tactics). Essentially, the legislation is trying to assure fairness. But even honest, informative promotion can run afoul of the law. A Halifax restaurant inadvertently violated the law when it said in its menu that its oat-bran muffins can reduce the risk of heart attacks. Oat bran can reduce serum cholesterol, and thus the risk of heart disease. Nonetheless, making that claim was illegal for the restaurateur.

REVIEW

After each promotion, you should evaluate its success in achieving your long-term and specific objectives. If you didn't achieve your goals, try to isolate the reasons. Did you promote the wrong product? Use the wrong medium? Was the amount of advertising appropriate for your goals? Was your timing off? Did you reach your target buyers? Was the message appropriate for them? Having these answers will help you fine-tune your strategy.

BANG FOR THE BUCK

Small businesses usually have limited marketing resources, so it's vital to get as much bang for your buck as possible. One way to do this is to make sure all your firm's communications reinforce one another, Derek Lackey suggests.

ESTABLISH AN IDENTITY

He recommends that new businesses visit a graphic designer to obtain a logo and letterhead design. "Most customers make decisions based on what they see. It starts with a company's letterhead and logo." The design should reflect the company's personality. "Most small businesses don't give enough thought to their firms' personality," he maintains. "You have to create it. It doesn't happen by accident. It's up to the owners to give a company its look, its feel, its personality." A good designer will ask questions about the firm and its customers, and create a logo that reflects its personality. "For example, a balloon shop should have a fun-looking logo," Lackey explains.

Having obtained the basic design, it should be used on all company communications: advertising, posters, letterhead, invoices, packaging, bags, direct mail, and even delivery trucks. "You need graphic consistency. Too often, a company's brochures, posters, and ads all look different," Lackey notes. By using the same graphic elements in all communications, a company continually reinforces its basic message.

An essential element of business identity is the company name. Lackey struggled for weeks to find a name for his firm before the lightbulb went on. His major draw was his own reputation; his company's activity was advertising; hence Lackey Advertising Inc. Victor Kokeram, whom we met in Chapter 2, continued to use the same name after he bought the NS Restaurant in 1985. He wondered why Caribbean food sold so well at his brother-in-law's restaurant, but not at his. There were many factors, but the name is undoubtedly one. His brother-in-law's restaurant is called The Caribbean Curry House, so patrons know exactly what to expect.

Japan Camera started in business in 1959 as Asa Camera, a pun on the owners' surname and the American Standards Association (ASA) scale used to rate the sensitivity of film to light. At that time, Japanese cameras were beginning to obtain a large share of the market. In 1960, Asa and his brothers capitalized on the growing awareness of Japanese cameras by renaming their business Japan Camera Centre. The result: an immediate increase in sales. "The name is important," Asa notes. "It has to suggest the business you're in." The firm reinforced the impression created by the name by clothing its sales people in distinctive red blazers with the company logo emblazoned on the vest pocket.

USE EVERY CENT OF CO-OP
Many suppliers offer co-op funds to retailers and distributors.

They'll pay a portion of advertising costs. Available funds are based on purchases. "Most small businesses don't use all the co-op money available to them," Lackey notes. "The amount of unused co-op money varies from industry to industry, but it's awesome." By not using co-op, retailers aren't just missing opportunities; they may be helping larger competitors. Lackey knows of firms that give unused co-op money to large customers who do use it. Most suppliers issue guidelines for the type of advertising eligible for co-op. But many are willing to bend their regulations, and will sometimes even increase the co-op pot for specific promotions. "Bigger companies are less flexible, but small suppliers can be very flexible," Lackey elaborates. "The bottom line is that they want to move more product. The problem is that most people never ask. The worst they can do is say no, but they may say yes."

FREE PUBLICITY

You may be able to get free publicity from newspapers, and radio and TV stations, if you can think of an appropriate story angle. It may be a plant opening. There may be something unique about your product that merits coverage in specialized publications. Think about the media that might be interested in your story. You can try to contact the appropriate editor directly; since editors are busy people, a written announcement followed by a telephone call is a surer way to get results.

We've seen how Alacritous attracted attention from computer and office-automation magazines, as well as the business press. Scandinavian Record Import, the classical record distributor we met in Chapter 4, had no advertising budget when it first opened. So Greg Pastic sent copies of his records to radio stations that play classical music. The resulting air-play generated awareness for his labels among consumers and record retailers.

BARTERING

You may be able to stretch your promotional dollars by bartering your products for advertising. "A lot of barter and contra goes on in advertising," Lackey says. Computer suppliers sometimes swap equipment for advertising space in computer and business publications, for example.

CROSS-PROMOTIONS

If two companies promote each other in their advertising, both realize more benefits than if they advertised on their own. These co-operative efforts are known as "cross-promotions." The theory behind cross-promotions is simple. "They work by driving one business's traffic to another business," explains Miles Nadal, president of The MDC Group of Companies, a Toronto-based marketing communications firm. To work, the companies' customers must overlap demographically and geographically. And the promotions should offer something of perceived high value. Several small prizes work better than a single large prize.

Cross-promotions are usually conducted by large players such as oil companies and fast-food chains. But there's room for small business, Nadal says, either in conjunction with other small businesses or as participants in large companies' promotions.

For example, Super Foods, a fast-food restaurant in Ponoka, Alberta, participated in a cross-promotion with Mohawk Oil Co. Ltd. of Burnaby, B.C., during 1986. Customers filling up their tanks at Mohawk stations were awarded bonus points entitling them to discounts on a wide variety of merchandise. Some co-sponsors were large concerns, such as Philips Electronics Ltd. and Pentax Canada Inc. Some were small independents, such as Super Foods. Co-owner Linda Steinman says the promotion generated "a lot of advertising" as well as additional business.

For cross-promotions to work, the partners should be in complementary businesses and have similar target markets. Retailers of maternity wear and baby furniture would be perfect partners for a cross-promotion. But the tie-in doesn't have to be so direct. For a fee, a Toronto video-rental chain puts stickers promoting a pizza chain on its videocassette boxes.

SELLING

Most companies use some kind of personal selling to promote their product. Whatever the product, whoever the seller, whoever the customer, the selling process is much the same.

PROSPECTING

Retailers usually have to wait for customers to come into the store before the selling process begins. The point of advertising, of course, is to get them to come into the store. But sales people in other industries go after sales opportunities. They may find prospects in the Yellow Pages or industry directories. They may get referrals from existing customers. Microcolor Dispersions Ltd. of Toronto, a manufacturer of liquid concentrate for the paint and auto-parts industries, gets prospects from computer databases. After it received an order from a maker of costume jewellery, it searched an industrial database for other similar businesses, thereby generating several new leads.

After identifying potential customers, sales people can write or phone. The purpose at this stage is to generate enough interest to get the prospect to agree to an interview. You have to get to the point quickly or the prospect will lose interest.

APPROACH

The first few seconds of any sales encounter are critical. If you create a poor impression, you'll never overcome it. Create a positive impression, and the rest of the encounter will flow smoothly. A well-groomed, friendly, well-informed, enthusiastic sales person will create a positive impression. A sloppy, surly, ignorant one won't.

Your goal in the first few seconds is to stimulate a dialogue with the customer, and put him or her at ease; so your first few words are vital. If the customer is looking at a product, comment on the product, and wait for a reply. The customer may not be shopping for that product, but will likely tell you what he or she *is* looking for. You might comment on a special promotion, a new line, even the weather—anything to get a conversation going. Once you're conversing, introduce yourself and ask the customer's name. Repeat it to make sure you've got it right, and use it regularly through the sales encounter.

Generally, sales people make several kinds of mistakes at this stage. Sometimes they come on too weakly. They use the universal opener, "Can I help you?" and get the universal reply, "No thanks, just looking," after which they fade into the background. The result: no dialogue with the customer. Sometimes they come on too strongly, with an opener such as, "What can I sell you today?" The result: an ill-at-ease customer looking for an opportunity to escape. Sometimes sales people drip with phony sincerity. The result: a suspicious customer. Sometimes they don't come on at all. They're too busy talking on the phone or doing paperwork to look after what should be their first priority: their customer. The result: a lost sales opportunity.

QUALIFICATION

Having stimulated a dialogue with the customer, you must determine his or her needs. Why does he or she want the product? How is he or she going to use it? What price is he or she willing to pay? What are his or her preferences, as to colour or size or style, for example?

The goal is to determine what products to demonstrate, and what will motivate the customer to buy them. That information will prove critical later in the sale. In some cases, you won't have a product that meets your customer's needs. As Japan Camera's Asa notes, no business can be all things to all people. If you can't solve your customer's problem, direct him or her to someone who can. You won't make this sale anyway, but the goodwill you generate may create future sales.

Common mistakes at this stage can be summarized under a single heading: *not listening*. The sales person may just assume that the customer is looking for the least-expensive product. If the customer wants a better-quality product, the sale is lost. And even if the sale is made, an opportunity for a higher-profit sale may be lost. Often, sales people have their own strong product preferences, and believe all people share them, or should. Again, the penalty for this kind of arrogance is a lost sales opportunity. Sometimes, sales people push customers into products with a sales incentive attached. They may make the sale, but if the product isn't what the customer needs, they're asking for after-sale headaches.

PRESENTATION

Having determined your customer's needs and motivation, the next step is to show products that meet them. You should emphasize your products' strengths and unique qualities. Explain their features and benefits in terms the customer can understand. If possible, let your customer play with the product. Show how it works.

Frequently, sales people emphasize features rather than benefits. A video sales person might tell the customer that a camcorder has autofocus. For a non-technical customer, this is useless information unless the sales person also explains that autofocus frees the user from having to refocus continuously, allowing him or her to concentrate on the subject. The benefit is clearly focused, more interesting videos. Equally common is failing to demonstrate the product's features. Some sales people are so consumed by their product they believe the customer should know as much about it as they do, and look down on buyers who aren't informed. In all these cases, the result is a bewildered or suspicious customer with no idea why he or she should buy the product.

CLOSING

If you've made your customer comfortable, determined his or her needs, shown a product that meets those needs, and explained its benefits in terms the customer can relate to, then he or she should be ready to buy. But a little nudge will help.

Depending on your selling style, you might simply ask if the customer wants to buy the product. If you favour a stronger selling style, you might pose a question that demands a favourable response, such as "Do you want to take it with you, or do you want it delivered?" "Do you want to pay by cash or credit card?" Some strong-arm types may just produce a blank invoice, and ask for information such as name and address.

Regardless of your closing question and closing style, the next step is the same: don't say a word. The silence at this stage can be overwhelming for both customer and sales person. If you say anything, you defeat the whole point of the exercise: to force the customer to make a decision.

One of two things will happen. Often, the customer will agree to buy the product. If you've determined your customer's needs and offered a product that meets those needs, then you're both winners. If the customer turns you down, and doesn't explain why, ask. Depending on the reason, you may just have to let him or her walk, and hope he or she will come back. On a high-ticket item, the customer may have to involve a spouse in the decision. An industrial client may have to get approval from superiors.

Some sales people apply too much pressure at this stage, alienating the customer. But the opposite failing is far more common. Too many sales people don't try to close at all. If the customer doesn't offer to buy after the presentation, they don't take any action. Willingness to close a sale is what distinguishes a sales person from an order-taker.

OVERCOMING OBJECTIONS

Often, the customer will raise objections that you can counter. This may occur during the presentation, or when you attempt to close. The customer may be uncertain as to whether the product really meets his or her needs. You have to go back to the presentation stage, explain the product and its benefits more clearly, then try to close again. Perhaps the product doesn't meet the customer's needs. You may not have delved deeply enough during the qualification stage; or the customer may not have revealed enough information. Regardless of the cause, you should requalify, demonstrate a product that meets the customer's needs, then try to close.

Sometimes the objections have nothing to do with the product.

The customer may want to shop around for a better price, or may be temporarily strapped for cash. You may have business policies, such as a money-back guarantee or interest-free credit, that can overcome those objections. You should point these out.

For some buyers, parting with hard-earned money is a painful process, particularly if they're unsure about what they're getting in return. Objections are sometimes a way of avoiding the purchase decision. Whatever the reason, your goal at this stage is to make your customer as comfortable as possible.

Common mistakes include dismissing the customer's objections rather than addressing them. The result: heightened suspicion. More often, the sales person just gives up, even though a simple explanation might be enough to overcome the objection and generate a sale.

SUGGESTION SELLING

Once the customer has made a decision, you may be able to convince him or her to buy complementary items. If a customer has bought a suit, he may need shirts, ties and a belt. If a customer has bought a camera, she may need film, a flashgun, a carrying case.

It's not always appropriate though. The customer may be traumatized by the purchase decision, and efforts to increase the sale may scare him or her off entirely.

But suggestion selling can make a real impact on the bottom line. Add-on items often have high margins, so they can increase profit more than their value would suggest. And they can increase customer satisfaction too, by making the purchase more useful.

FOLLOW-UP

Many sales people forget about the customer after they've made the sale. That's a mistake, for several reasons. First, you can determine whether the customer is happy with the purchase and, if not, you can take measures to address the problem. Word-of-mouth is the most persuasive form of advertising. A satisfied customer can generate new sales opportunities; an unhappy customer will hinder future sales.

Second, you may be able to generate additional sales by informing the customer of special promotions. You may be able to suggest accessories that complement the original purchase. Finally, you may be able to get referrals to other potential customers.

The objective at this stage is to develop an ongoing relationship with the customer, to turn a single sale into a continuing source of revenue. The most common mistake among sales people is not following up at all.

THE MARKETING MIX

What a business does about product, place, pricing and promotion defines its "marketing mix." Obviously, all of the four Ps are interdependent. A "destination" retailer in an out-of-the-way location will have to advertise more than a retailer in a high-traffic mall. He or she will have to give some reason, such as a low price, for customers to shop at his or her store. By contrast, the mall retailer is putting his or her marketing dollars into higher store rents instead of advertising, into "place" rather than "promotion." A retailer in an upscale neighbourhood will carry a different product mix and have a different pricing strategy than a retailer in a middle-class neighbourhood.

Alacritous Inc.'s marketing strategies illustrate this interdependence. It introduced Alacrity at $2,000 in order to get the software into businesses, but within a year raised the price to $4,500 after clients said they thought the product was underpriced. Several factors influenced its pricing moves. A high price, for example, $25,000, would have lengthened the sales cycle unacceptably, and would have limited its markets. The company was targeting large buyers who would purchase multiple copies. This wouldn't have been possible with a high price. But a price of a few hundred dollars would have precluded direct selling and forced Alacritous to rely on retailers and distributors. Extensive advertising would have been needed to build awareness and demand for the product. Alacritous didn't have the promotion budget for this. From a competitive standpoint, the $4,500 price made sense. The program didn't have any direct competition, although consultants are a form of indirect competition. Alacrity costs the same as two days of a strategic consultant's services, so the payback is very short.

The marketing mix isn't arrived at arbitrarily. It's based on the business type, goals, market segment and image. If you haven't established these, it's impossible to mount an effective marketing campaign. How can you choose product, establish pricing, select a location or plan promotion if you don't know what you're selling, or to whom you're selling, or what your long-term goals are, or what image you're trying to convey?

It's not hard to find examples of the influence of customer profile on a company's marketing mix. For furniture and appliance stores, an important market is recent home-buyers. While they need furniture and appliances for their new homes, these customers are usually strapped for cash. Many successful merchants offer extended credit terms at no interest to attract these cash-starved buyers. These terms are heavily promoted in their advertising. The financing charges are considered part of the store's overhead and are included in product prices. Many of the firms offering these terms are very large, so the cost of these promotions is offset to a large degree by their buying power. But even if they have to pass on some of the financing charges in the form of higher prices, for cash-shy new homeowners, the ability to buy a needed appliance and pay for it in six months is more appealing than a slightly lower cash price.

The marketing mix also has to take into account factors outside the entrepreneur's control. These include any laws and regulations that apply to your industry, labour supply, culture, competition and economic conditions. The entrepreneur must consider all these when formulating marketing plans. Rotenberg cites one example. Especially in Southern Ontario, retailers are affected by labour shortages. Taking low labour supply and high wage costs into account, a retailer might de-emphasize personal selling and put more money into advertising and self-serve displays. The Steals People, the office-equipment chain we met in Chapter 5, uses a combination of self-serve displays for low- and medium-priced goods such as books and computer software, complemented by personal selling for complex, high-priced goods such as computers and FAX machines.

For a marketing strategy to work, it has to be coherent. Despite their differences, successful companies such as Alacritous Inc., Japan Camera, Magnum Dynalab and The Steals People have one thing in common: their disciplined approach to marketing. The many elements of marketing—product, price, place, promotion, customer profile and external conditions—are like pieces in a jigsaw puzzle. If you put the pieces together properly, you create an appealing picture of your business. Customers know what you offer, and why they should do business with you. Assemble the pieces haphazardly, and there's no picture at all. Your customers will have no idea of what you do or what you offer, and no idea of why they should patronize your business. Planning makes the difference.

9/YOUR PROFESSIONAL PARTNERS:
Dealing with Accountants and Other Business Advisers

When Sybil Shore started her cosmetics business in 1981, she knew she'd need help with financial management. She got the help she needed from her accountant. As it turned out, Shore's relationship with her accountant worked exceptionally well.

A native of Nova Scotia, Shore had been working as a nurse at a Toronto hospital for several years. "By 1981, I was getting bored, and was looking for something else to do," she recalls. She was contemplating moving into pharmaceutical sales when a friend told her about a cosmetics franchising organization. The friend's sister-in-law had been successful with the company, and thought Shore ought to give it a try.

Shore was sceptical, but attended some meetings. To try out the concept, she sold part-time for one of the company's franchisees. "I made more money than I was making in nursing," she relates. "I knew I had found my niche. I enjoyed being with people who also wanted to go somewhere."

At that time, the franchisor was opening up Canadian territories, and was pushing Shore to make a commitment. She was unsure, and flew home to discuss the idea with her father. Shore was 26 and single at the time. "Most of the company's franchises are owned by husband-and-wife teams," she explains. "The wife looks after sales and image, while the husband is the administrator/manager. I didn't know if I could do it alone.

"My father believed in me. He saw something in me I didn't. He'd been in business all his life, and told me, 'Do it now. You won't do it later.'" Shore took his advice. Her new company, Halifax-based Aloette Cosmetics of Nova Scotia Ltd., purchased distribution rights for Nova Scotia, New Brunswick and Prince Edward Island for Aloette cosmetics. She paid $8,000 for her first batch of product, and agreed to pay the $50,000 franchise fee over time, based on her sales. The debt was paid off within a year.

Strong in marketing and sales, Shore knew she'd need help with the financial end of her business. Besides lacking a business background, she faced an additional problem: bankers were sceptical of her ability to manage a business. Rather than accepting startup money from her father, she sought a $10,000 line of credit from local banks. "The first bank manager sat across the desk laughing inside. He couldn't handle the fact that I was so confident and so exuberant."

Shore got the funding she needed from another bank, helped by her father's reputation in the community. And she had the last laugh. By 1989, Aloette of Nova Scotia was selling $1.5 million worth of cosmetics a year.

One of the factors that contributed to her success, she says, was "I hired a good accountant, someone I could ask stupid questions. He helped me understand cashflow, bank statements and other financial aspects of my business." He assisted her in her relations with her bank, and kept her informed about what was happening in her business. In her case, the relationship worked unusually well. She ended up marrying her accountant.

RELATIONS WITH PROFESSIONAL ADVISERS

Your accountant probably won't end up as your partner in life. Nonetheless, he or she can be a very important person in your business. So are other business advisers, such as lawyers and consultants. The right advisers can shore up weak areas in your own management skills.

In any new venture, money is always short. Owner/managers who cut corners on professional services can end up paying more than they save. Certainly, there are some jobs you or an employee can do more cheaply than a professional. You might save some money by doing your own books or producing your own financial statements. But good advice from an accountant might save you thousands of dollars on taxes.

REFERENCES

As with other important business decisions, the choice of professional advisers must be made carefully. Consider Gordon Hunter's experience. In 1982, he retained an accountant to computerize his company's accounting system. The consultant, whom Hunter knew casually before retaining him, was given total responsibility for the system, right down to hiring an operator. Unknown to Hunter, the consultant had little prior experience with computers. In effect, he was learning at Hunter's expense.

The results were catastrophic. Instead of analysing the company's needs and finding appropriate software and hardware, the consultant bought products with which he was already familiar. When the operator was unable to obtain important financial information from the computer, she was fired, and the consultant hired as a controller. He didn't fare any better. Receivables and payables were a mess. Some bills were paid twice, some not at all. Some invoices were never sent out. It took days to get such routine information as bank balances. Finally, the consultant was fired and a new controller hired on the recommendation of the firm's auditors. After reverting to a manual system, it took him a year to clean up the company's records.

Reflects Hunter: "A little knowledge is dangerous. Our consultant knew enough about accounting and computers to tell a good story. He was a glib, fast-talking guy who said what we wanted to hear." The lesson: before retaining a professional adviser, get references and check them out.

SELECTING ADVISERS

Selecting a professional adviser is similar in many ways to hiring an employee, which we covered in Chapter 7. Just as you'll hire more effectively if you develop a job description before screening employees, you'll fare better if you list all your needs before you choose advisers and evaluate them against this list.

Having determined your needs and budget, think about the qualifications the adviser should have. Consider the individual's experience. If you require specialized advice, weigh the person's background in that specific area. Also weigh the person's experience with owner-managed business and your industry. You may also want to consider the person's academic and professional credentials.

THE INITIAL INTERVIEW

The purpose of the interview is similar to a job interview: for client and candidate to assess the candidate's suitability for the task at hand. To that end, you should elicit information about the professional's experience and credentials and, where possible, obtain references.

Many professionals will grant an initial meeting at no charge, or a very small one, to discuss the client's needs. Fees should be frankly and fully discussed in the initial interview, something any reputable professional should be willing to do. It's then up to you to weigh the professional's qualifications and fees, bearing in mind your own needs.

To help professionals estimate costs and the ability to address your needs, you should come to the meeting with appropriate documents. And as with any important meeting, you should prepare a list of questions beforehand.

It's rare that a business will interview just one candidate for a position. Similarly, it's not a good idea to interview a single lawyer, accountant or other professional. As with employee-hiring, make a shortlist of qualified candidates, then interview several. By interviewing at least three, you'll get an idea of the choices available. And you'll probably get different, and possibly valuable, insights into your own business situation.

WORKING WITH ADVISERS

Not only do you want to find someone qualified and someone you can afford, you want to find an adviser you're comfortable with. "If you're intimidated by your lawyer, as many people are, the relationship won't work," observes Toronto litigation lawyer Jerry Levitan. The same is true of relationships with other professionals.

These relationships call for trust on both sides. For the relationships to work, you should be as frank as possible in your discussions with professional advisers. And you should expect them to keep confidential information confidential.

You'll be relying on your adviser, so look for someone whose judgment you can trust. At times, that may involve recommending someone else for a job that is beyond the scope of the individual adviser.

Courtesy is also required. You should expect any professional adviser to return your phone calls promptly. Remember, however, that these people have other clients, so can't respond to every request immediately. Courtesy cuts both ways. You should respond quickly to requests for information or instructions from your advisers. They can't help you without your co-operation.

You may find at some point that the relationship isn't working. Or you might want a second opinion on some complex matter. In either case, you're entitled to seek the services of another professional. Your adviser should be willing to send your files to whomever you direct.

As with employees and suppliers, you should be in charge of your relations with professional and business advisers. However, you should remember that you're paying for their experience and judgment. It's up to you to apply their judgment to your business decisions.

SELECTING AN ACCOUNTANT

You can get referrals for accountants from bankers, lawyers, other owner/managers, or you can find names in the Yellow Pages. The professional bodies that govern accountants will also give referrals.

As Shore's experience confirms, a good accountant can help compensate for weaknesses in financial management. As well as answering routine questions, he or she can serve as a sounding-board for your ideas. Your accountant can help smooth relations with your bank manager, as Shore found. If your business plan and other documents have been reviewed by your accountant, they'll carry more weight at the bank. Your accountant will be able to help you prepare cashflow projections, so that you know ahead of time how much money you'll need. You'll get a much more sympathetic hearing if you inform your bank manager about your cash needs well ahead of time, rather than asking for an increased line of credit to meet tomorrow's payroll.

As we saw in Chapter 6, it's vital to get regular financial information about your business in order to make good, informed decisions. If you don't have internal personnel to maintain books and produce regular statements, your accounting firm should be able to provide this service. The right accountant will be able to spot trouble signs – rising expenses or sliding sales, for example. That way, you can solve the problem before it becomes a crisis. Without good information, a business can find itself in serious trouble, as we'll see in Chapter 11. And by structuring your business affairs properly, a capable accountant may save you thousands of dollars in income taxes.

Different businesses will have different needs, and different budgets. Accountants usually charge by the hour; but their rates may vary according to the service offered. A lower rate is usually charged for routine bookkeeping or for preparation of statements than for tax advice. Some businesses employ part-time or full-time bookkeepers for day-to-day record-keeping, and a professional accountant for producing statements and giving advice on complex business matters. Others use their accounting firm as a one-stop service, for everything from bookkeeping to consulting to tax-return preparation.

When shopping for accounting services, look for someone who understands your type of business. Look for someone who anticipates problems, rather than someone who simply reacts to your questions. Look for someone who takes an interest in your business, rather than someone who just shows you how to keep books. Your accountant should complete your tax return well before the deadline, and tell you when to make instalments so as to avoid interest and penalties. He or she should inform you about tax changes that affect your business, and suggest ways of reacting to them.

There is a tremendous range of accounting firms serving independent business. These range from small independent operators working out of their homes to national firms with offices across Canada. Large and medium-sized firms supply a complete range of accounting services. And many offer consulting services to address other management needs. If you need advice on computers or personnel management, a large firm will usually be able to provide it. You can also obtain these services from firms specializing in these areas.

CHOOSING A BANKER

Strictly speaking, your banker isn't a professional adviser. Businesses use banks for financing, cheque-processing and other services. You can replace professional advisers if the relationship isn't working. But with your banker, the shoe's on the other foot. However, bankers can sometimes provide valuable business advice.

We covered some elements of the banking relationship in Chapter 3. There, we noted the advantages of dealing with a commercial rather than a consumer banker. A commercial branch, particularly one that specializes in independent business, can offer services tailored to your needs. The manager is probably more accustomed to dealing with business credit applications, and may have a higher approval ceiling. Ideally, the account manager will have some experience in your industry.

THE BANKING RELATIONSHIP

You should make it a point to keep your banker informed about your business, suggests Gerry LeJan, manager of The Royal Bank of Canada's independent business centre in downtown Toronto. "That may mean getting together with your account manager two to four times a year. If your sales are up, you might include a note with your month-end list of inventory and receivables. If you come across a magazine article that might help the account manager understand your industry, send it to him. It's easier to deal with a client if you know the industry."

Account managers are supposed to make periodical visits to clients' places of business. "If your account manager isn't visiting, invite him or her to look at your operation," LeJan advises. "It's important for the account manager to make sure there are boxes on the shelves. But a visit also helps the manager understand the business. It's useful to meet key personnel, such as the bookkeeper. That way, he or she doesn't have to talk to the owner every time a question comes up. And meeting the key people helps him or her to get a feel for the strengths and weaknesses of the business."

TURNOVER

Unlike other key people, you can't exactly choose your own banker. You have some choice when you first choose a bank. Partly to prevent relationships between account managers and borrowers from becoming too close, banks usually rotate account managers every few years. That means you have to go through the work of establishing relationships with your new account manager: briefing them on your business and industry and getting to know them.

This is a major sore point between small business and banks, says Catherine Swift, chief economist for the Canadian Federation of Independent Business. "With a new manager, you're back to square one. The new person may impose new things on the business." Sometimes a new account manager will demand additional security or increase interest requirements. Sometimes he or she will introduce new service charges. Swift tells of one business whose borrowing terms were radically altered after a new bank manager took over its account. Prior to the change, it could draw on its line of credit and pay it down in $1,000 increments. The new manager increased the minimum draw and paydown to $5,000. That resulted in a significant increase in interest payments, since the business sometimes had to draw more money than it needed, and had to keep the money outstanding for longer periods. In this case, the owner/manager went to another bank.

LeJan acknowledges that changes in account managers can be difficult, but maintains that real horror stories are rare. "There's a strain when any relationship changes. It's no different with an account manager than with a doctor or dentist. Most banks try to make the change as smoothly as possible. They'll introduce the manager to the client, and try to maintain continuity in other positions so that the client doesn't feel like an orphan."

Sometimes changes can have positive results, he adds. "It's an opportunity to the bank and the client to refresh the relationship. The new manager may have seen ideas that worked well elsewhere, or may have some challenging questions about the business, or may be able to offer new facilities."

INSURANCE BROKERS

Businesses face a great number of risks, and an equal number of insurance products to help them manage those risks. The first step in risk management is to identify your risks. They may include fire, with consequent damage to building, equipment, inventory and other assets; death or illness of key personnel; liability for injury to employees, customers or other parties; theft and fraud; loss of business income resulting from fire or other calamity; bad debts.

After evaluating the risks you'll face in your business, you have to decide how to handle them. You might accept some as a fact of life and take action to minimize others. Locking up expensive items and installing alarm systems are ways of minimizing the risk of theft, for example. But there are some risks businesses can't afford to take: fires, for example. The way to handle these risks is to transfer them to another party by purchasing insurance.

Property insurance will protect covered assets against specified perils, such as fire, flood and theft. Business-interruption insurance will protect you against loss of income resulting from specified perils. Liability insurance will cover you if you're sued for specific acts or omissions. Life and disability insurance protects you against the death or disability of key people. Business-continuation insurance provides money for the business or other partners to purchase the shares from the estate of a deceased partner.

Often, businesses are required to have specific types of insurance by banks or landlords. Companies may be required to post surety bonds guaranteeing their fulfilment of a contract. Construction companies, for example, often have to post bonds guaranteeing that a project will be finished on time and on budget. If the job is late or over-budget, the bonding company pays the amount of the bond to the contractor's client.

When planning a risk-management program, identify your greatest risks and insure them first. With each risk, you should consider the amount of loss you can afford to absorb, and try to find a policy with a corresponding deductible amount. That will help control costs.

In addition to transferring business risks, employers may wish to provide dental, disability, life and other forms of insurance to employees as part of their benefits package.

Insurance can be purchased from brokers who represent several different companies or by agents who work directly for a single insurer. A well-connected independent broker should be able to provide all the insurance products you need. You may be able to save money with direct agents, as commission costs are usually lower. If you deal with an agent, make sure he or she provides the kind of coverage you require. As with other professionals, consider the broker's professional credentials and experience in your industry. Ask for referrals from other businesses and professionals. Look for someone who will perform a thorough analysis of your business; and who will be there if you have to make a claim.

As with other business expenses, it's worthwhile getting competitive quotes for insurance. As well as cost, compare thoroughness of coverage. Saving a few dollars on premiums will be cold comfort if the insurer fails to cover a loss. Your accountant can help you evaluate the insurer's financial reserves, record at handling claims and restrictions it places on your coverage.

OTHER ADVISERS

Owner/managers will often lack the knowledge necessary to make decisions that vitally affect their businesses. Sometimes they can address the knowledge gap by studying the area, or by asking colleagues with the necessary experience for help. But sometimes it can be helpful to call in a consultant.

Businesses may be able to get help from small-business counsellors with the federal and provincial governments. Some large municipalities also offer this kind of service, as do the business schools of many universities and colleges. Under its Counselling Assistance for Small Enterprises (CASE) program, the Federal Business Development Bank (FBDB) offers consulting services on a wide variety of issues, using retired business people.

Private consultants are available to help with technical problems, such as installing computers or phone systems. Others can help with marketing, financial or personnel issues. Most professional consultants bill by the hour. As noted, many of these consulting services are available through accounting firms.

Unlike most business professionals, there are no governing bodies for consultants. Because anyone can hang out a consultant's shingle, it's especially important to check the reputation of the firm and individual consultant. As Gordon Hunter learned, an incapable consultant can wreak havoc on a company. Look for someone with experience in your industry. Ask whether the consultant performed tasks effectively and on time. Get competitive quotes. And provide your consultant with all the information he or she needs to do the job.

Those rules apply to all professionals. You shouldn't expect, or allow, them to make your business decisions for you. That's especially true when dealing with lawyers, a subject we'll discuss in the next chapter. But if you choose and use them wisely, professional advisers can help you make better decisions.

10/BUSINESS AND THE LAW:
"The Best Legal Decision May Not Be the Best Business Decision"

In December 1986, Edward Borins was preparing to celebrate victory in his three-year battle with the Ontario government over Sunday shopping. Since 1983, Toronto-based Edwards Books & Art had been open Sundays and many holidays, and had been charged 300 times under Ontario's Retail Business Holidays Act (RBHA). After numerous trials and appeals, his case had reached the Supreme Court of Canada. His lawyer was arguing that the act violated religious-freedom guarantees in the Charter of Rights, and Borins expected that the court would rule in his favour.

While waiting for the court's decision, Borins remarked to another lawyer how relieved he was that his legal nightmare would soon be over. Toronto litigation lawyer Jerry Levitan had acted on behalf of a Toronto video rental chain charged under the RBHA and had won at the Ontario Court of Appeal; he was present at Borins's Supreme Court trial as an observer.

"He told me I didn't have a chance," Borins says and recalls that he was devastated. The numerous charges and court appearances had been emotionally draining for Borins and his staff. He had spent more than $100,000 on legal fees. Paying fines on 300 convictions would probably put him out of business. Levitan suggested to Borins that he lobby the Ontario government to exempt bookstores from the act, just as entertainment outlets and magazine stores are exempt.

As it turned out, Levitan was right. The Supreme Court ruled against Borins and his co-defendants. The Retail Business Holidays Act does violate the Charter, the court said, but the government is nonetheless entitled to establish a common pause day.

However, the story ended happily for Borins. He joined with other booksellers, and they persuaded the Ontario government to amend the act. Borins isn't a full-fledged supporter of Sunday shopping, but maintains that bookstores are different from most retail operations. "People do enjoy a common pause day, but it's discriminating against intellectuals to keep bookstores closed when sporting events, video stores and movie theatres can open on Sundays. We asked for consistency in the area of recreation. The act says that any business open for recreational, educational or amusement purposes is exempt." Borins found that many individuals and groups who oppose Sunday shopping supported an exemption for bookstores. Under a private member's bill passed in June 1987, bookstores and art galleries were permitted to open Sundays and holidays. After the bill was passed, Borins paid a nominal fine for his convictions under the RBHA.

"In retrospect, it was a terrible error on my part to challenge the act," he reflects. Throughout his three-year court battle, Borins's lawyers had assured him he had a good chance of winning. "Thank God I found a lawyer with the guts to say I'm not going to win, who wasn't out for money or an ego trip." He calls his long legal battle "a nightmare. I became a victim of lawyers who forget about their clients."

Lawyers aren't necessarily out to fleece their clients, Levitan says, but often they don't act in their clients' best interests. "A litigation lawyer's natural response is to go to court," he explains. "If a client has a problem, a lawyer's response is to seek injunctions, to sue, to file motions, without looking at what will best serve the client. But the best legal decision may not be the best business decision."

He compares Borins's court battle with the myth of Sisyphus, the legendary king condemned to the eternal labour of rolling a large stone up a hill, only to see it fall to the plain below. "It was the right cause, but the wrong fight. Responding to the charges and paying the fines could have put him out of business."

Several lessons can be gleaned from Borins's experience. The chief one is the need for businesses to choose professional advisers carefully — not just lawyers, but accountants, bankers, consultants and other professionals. Another is the need to consider the effect of their advice on your business. Yet another is that there are several means to the same end.

Levitan says, in elaboration, "Lawyers respond to legal issues, but their first question should be: 'How can the client accomplish what he or she wants?' Is the best way to spend $100,000 in legal fees, or is there an easier approach? In this case, we found it easier to lobby."

POTENTIAL PROBLEMS

Businesses get involved in litigation for many reasons, Levitan says. Sometimes, as in Borins's case, the business runs afoul of the law and gets into trouble with the government. Sometimes the problem involves another business, sometimes an employee.

Disputes between partners are very frequent, he says. As we noted in Chapter 1, a well-drafted partnership or shareholder agreement may not eliminate disputes between business partners, but it makes them easier to resolve.

Other common problems include breach of contract. A customer may have bloated inventory, and refuse to accept goods he or she has committed to buy. A franchisee may not be aware of hidden costs, and balk at paying them.

NON-PAYMENT

Another common problem is non-payment. "Usually it's a function of a buyer's financial problems," Levitan comments, "but it's remarkable the extent to which people use non-payment to finance their businesses. Some are incredibly adept at this. They *want* to be sued. They'll concoct an inane defence and keep you tied up for years."

Prevention is the best way to address this problem. As noted in Chapter 6, thorough credit checks will usually reveal this kind of operator before you grant credit. However, this is cold comfort if you're stuck with a bad debt. What do you do then?

It depends on the amount, Levitan says. "If it's under $10,000, you're crazy to have litigation. Maybe you'll just have your lawyer send the debtor a demand letter." An alternative is to sue in Small Claims Court, where businesses can represent themselves rather than hiring a lawyer. Bear in mind that there is a maximum claim allowed in Small Claims Court, and it varies depending on the jurisdiction. In Toronto, it's $3,000. If you're trying to recover a $6,000 debt, it might be better to sue the debtor for $3,000 in Small Claims Court than to try to recover the whole debt.

UNJUST DISMISSAL

Many owner/managers underestimate the potential problems of

firing an employee, Levitan says. If someone isn't working out, most employers phone their provincial Employment Standards office to determine the appropriate amount of wages and vacation pay. "They think that's all they have to pay."

Theoretically, they may be right. But practically, they're setting themselves up for an unjust-dismissal lawsuit, something Levitan calls "the fender-bender of the '80s and '90s. Rarely is someone fired without someone else telling him or her about a lawyer who can get him or her some money from the ex-employer. The lawyer tells the ex-employee that the law imposes minimum requirements on the employer, but that he or she might be able to get a year's pay plus damages for mental distress."

Unjust-dismissal suits can be prevented if you handle the dismissal properly. If you know you're going to have to fire someone, it's a good idea to speak to a labour lawyer first, Levitan advises. Consulting a labour lawyer is absolutely essential if your business is unionized. The lawyer will help you work out a cost-efficient way of handling the dismissal. He or she will probably recommend that you give the employee an opportunity to correct the problem. A written memo should spell out the areas of difficulty. The employee should be told that if the problem isn't corrected in a month, his or her employment will be reviewed. If the problem persists, you should ask the person how long it will take him or her to find another job, then work out a settlement. It may involve a lump-sum payment, payments spread out over time, or a period during which the employee continues to work for the firm. Explains Levitan: "The goal is to protect yourself by giving the employee an opportunity to mitigate damages resulting from the dismissal."

HUMAN-RIGHTS COMPLAINTS

Rather than suing, some dismissed employees file complaints with the provincial or federal human-rights commissions, alleging racial, sexual or religious discrimination. This tactic has real advantages for the complainant. For one thing, he or she doesn't need a lawyer, since the commission acts on the complainant's behalf. (That's true everywhere except B.C., where the complainant's and respondent's rights are more fairly balanced.)

The offence may be genuine, or it may be trivial. "If the complaint is upheld, the commission may award damages for not only discrimination but wrongful dismissal – maybe one year's salary – plus punitive damages that the courts might not award," Levitan explains. "The Ontario Human Rights Code is a remarkable means to get money from an employer just for making a joke." The situation is similar in most other provinces, he adds.

And the system is stacked against the employer. A single body acts as the complainant's lawyer, investigator, judge and jury. Normal judicial rules of evidence and burdens of proof are not observed by human-rights commissions. Comments Levitan: "The system is open to severe abuse. Some employees know they can extort money from employers by threatening to lodge complaints."

To prevent this kind of problem, employers should be aware of the consequences of discrimination, including an inappropriate joke or comment.

COMPETITION ACT VIOLATIONS

Levitan says the federal Department of Consumer and Corporate Affairs (CCA) is becoming more aggressive in its application of the misleading advertising provisions of the Competition Act. "We're seeing increasing charges against small businesses where the violation isn't serious. A small store may advertise sale prices on 40 items, most of which are accurate. But on one or two, the prices may be close to what they were before the sale. Usually it's a mistake or an advertising error. The customer buys the item, sees it two weeks later for the same price and lodges a complaint. A couple of weeks later, an investigator shows up with a 20-page summons."

Minor violations used to be handled quickly with nominal fines, Levitan says. "Now there's a strong inclination to prosecute and convict people who 'mislead.' " Fighting the charge may involve a two-week trial, with corresponding legal costs. "Often the best advice is to plead guilty and accept the fine." The fine, even for a minor violation, might be as high as $5,000, he warns. Besides the fine, there are other risks associated with a guilty plea. "A guilty plea results in a conviction being recorded, and next time you'll get a bigger whack."

You can take steps to prevent these problems. First of all, keep your advertising and sale practices honest. "There are going to be people watching you: your customers and your competitors," Levitan advises. "If you play with fire, you're going to get burned." It also pays to develop a relationship with the local CCA office. If you're worried about a specific ad, show it to an officer and get an opinion. "At least they'll see you're trying," he notes.

LITIGATION

No matter how careful you are, you're probably going to have legal problems at some point. You may be prosecuted by the government for a genuine or trivial offence, you may be sued by someone justifiably or unjustifiably. Or perhaps you'll be wronged and want to sue – perhaps by a customer refusing to pay a large bill; perhaps by a partner in a joint venture reneging on an agreement. Whatever the situation, your first instinct may be to fight back as hard as you can.

Before acting, Levitan says you should look at what's involved in litigation. "When clients want to sue, I give a speech about the extent to which things can go wrong, and the extent to which they might have to pay. If someone's looking at costs of $15,000 to deal with a $30,000 dispute, he or she sees the light pretty quickly."

THE LITIGATION PROCESS

As Borins discovered, the litigation process is long and complex, and costs climb very quickly. The plaintiff's lawyer drafts a writ of summons and statement of claim, in which the plaintiff's allegations are listed and a claim for damages made. These papers are filed with the court and served on the defendant. The defendant's lawyer then prepares a statement of defence, outlining the case from the client's viewpoint. The defendant may also file a counterclaim against the plaintiff, in effect becoming a plaintiff in a second lawsuit. For example, a defendant being sued for non-payment may sue for damages resulting from defective goods. The two lawyers give each other a list of documents being used in the case, and if requested, copies of the documents. During discovery, plaintiff and defendant are examined under oath by their opponent's lawyer. Before the trial date is set, there may be a pre-trial conference between the parties' lawyers and the judge. Then there's the trial itself, where each lawyer examines witnesses, cross-examines opponent's witnesses and presents his or her case. The judge or jury then decides who's responsible for the problem, and how much the plaintiff should be paid. Either party can appeal the decision or the amount of the award. If the appeal is allowed, the case will be tried again in a higher court. Once a judgment is handed down, the winner determines the loser's assets, and if possible, collects on the judgment.

RISKS

In addition to the time involved in the procedures themselves, lawyers have to spend time on research and preparation. During the process, lawyers may file motions on legal procedures, lengthening the process. An opponent may use delaying tactics to induce the other side to settle. An opponent with deep pockets might stretch proceedings out, hoping you'll give up. All the while, the meter is ticking at a cost of hundreds of dollars per hour. On top of that, there are other costs, such as the lawyer's out-of-pocket expenses and fees for expert witnesses. If you win, the other party may have to pay some of your costs; if you lose, you'll have to do the same. Of course, if you win, you also have to collect. This could prove difficult if, for example, the losing firm lacks the assets to cover your judgment.

On top of the expense, litigation consumes a great deal of time. It can take years for a lawsuit to be resolved. Owners and key management may have to be present at a lengthy trial and at discoveries. In addition, there's inevitable emotional turmoil, which takes your attention away from your business. The other side will be taking its best shot. As well as presenting its case as strongly as possible, it will attempt to trivialize your case.

Sometimes you'll have no choice but to fight. The other party may insist on seeing the lawsuit through to the end, or the opposition's lawyer may manipulate him or her in that direction. "That happens quite a lot," Levitan says. "If it does, you've got to hope you have a good lawyer. It pays to have a very good litigation lawyer. If he or she has a reputation, he or she may ask for a stiff retainer. You might find someone else who charges half, then find he or she is being eaten alive by the other side."

But often, it's possible to have your lawyer work out a settlement with your opponent's lawyer. "This can be the best course, even if it involves a significant reduction in what you're owed," Levitan says. As he's already noted, you should make the best *business* decision when contemplating legal action.

STARTUP ISSUES

Businesses don't need lawyers just when they're in some kind of legal difficulty. Just as it's less painful to prevent illness than cure it, it's less expensive to *prevent* legal problems than it is to *solve* them.

Terence Dobbin, a corporate/commercial lawyer with Osler, Hoskin & Harcourt, deals with companies in the startup phase. He says it's vital for entrepreneurs to talk to lawyers in the early stages of business formation about fundamental issues such as corporate structure, shareholders' and partnership agreements, financing, trade marks and patents.

"Think about how you're going to carry on business, and how you're going to protect yourself from competitors and creditors. For example, if you're looking for partners, there's a fine line between what you should and shouldn't reveal. A non-disclosure agreement will help you shut the door before the horses escape."

INCORPORATION

Key startup issues include company structure, and shareholder and partnership agreements, both of which we touched on in Chapter 1. "The decision of whether or not to incorporate is tax-driven to a large extent," Dobbin says. The other factor in the decision is limited liability. Ordinarily, shareholders are not personally liable for a corporation's debts. "Limited liability is a very nice concept, but the fact of the matter is that most startups have to give personal guarantees to get financing," Dobbin notes, "so limited liability is a bit illusory. But it does help to protect you from trade creditors."

If you decide to incorporate, you'll also have to decide whether to incorporate federally or provincially. Federally incorporated companies face greater professional costs and more stringent reporting requirements than provincial companies. Some businesses, such as radio stations, must incorporate federally. Your decision should also be informed by your long-term plans. A retailer who hopes to become a national chain has different objectives than one who plans to maintain a single location. These are the kinds of issues you should address in your initial discussions with your lawyer, Dobbin notes. "He or she will sit down with you and help you focus your goals, then help you implement your decision."

COMPANY NAME

After choosing a name for your company, you have to ensure that no one's already using it, or a similar one. You or your lawyer can arrange a name search with the appropriate provincial ministry or computer database service. If you use a name identical or one similar to that used by another business, that business may be able to force you to stop using the name and sue for damages. A name search is inexpensive. Changing your business's name once it's established, and obtaining new invoices, letterhead, business cards and outdoor signs costs a lot more. A partnership or proprietorship simply registers its name with the appropriate provincial agency. A corporation's name is registered when it's incorporated. Sometimes corporations will operate under a different name from their corporate one, in which case the trade name should be registered with the appropriate provincial agency.

Trade Marks

In addition to your company or trade name, your company may have trade marks associated with its products. Trade marks can include words or phrases, logos, designs, distinctive packaging or product design or a combination of these. As long as your trade mark doesn't conflict with those of other companies, you can use it. But registering it under the Trade Marks Act will provide increased protection in case other companies use the same trade mark, or one similar enough to cause confusion in your market. Providing you're actively using your trade mark, once registered your protection lasts 15 years (it's renewable after that) and extends to all of Canada. Should someone infringe on your trade mark, you have more legal options than if the mark is unregistered. Companies contemplating using a similar trade mark will, one hopes, see yours in the trade mark registry and choose a different mark. In addition, registering your trade marks in Canada makes it easier to register them in other countries, and to license them to third parties, such as franchisees. To protect your trade marks, the names' registered users should be filed with the Trade Marks Office.

Patents

If you've developed a unique and useful new product or process, you may be able to patent it. If you disclose your invention (say, in radio interviews or tradeshow exhibits), you must apply for a patent within a year. (This "grace period" varies from country to country. In many nations, disclosure makes the invention unpatentable in that country.) It's prudent to conduct a preliminary search to confirm that the invention is patentable. For example, if a similar invention is already protected by patent, it may not be worthwhile to proceed with your application. In the patent application, the applicant describes the invention and outlines his claims, that is the scope of the patent. The goal is to describe the invention narrowly enough to distinguish it from previous ones, but broadly enough to discourage new competition. Once approved, a patent bars others from exploiting your idea for 18 years. But it's up to you to enforce it.

COPYRIGHT

Original artistic or cultural works, such as books, music, paintings, films and photographs, are protected by copyright. No one may publish, reproduce, perform or otherwise use the work (or large parts of it) without the permission of the copyright owner. Copyright lasts for the life of the author, plus 50 years. On reproduced material, such as records and tapes, copyright lasts for 50 years from the original recording. In Canada, copyright is automatically granted to the creator of an original work, providing the creator is a Canadian citizen or a citizen of a country that adheres to the International Copyright Convention. The copyright can be sold outright to another party, or specific rights (say, first Canadian publication) can be assigned or licensed. Copyright can be registered with the copyright office for a nominal fee.

INDUSTRIAL DESIGN

The design for a manufactured product with a distinctive shape, pattern or ornamentation can be protected under the Industrial Design Act. To be protected, the design must be registered with the Industrial Design Registry within one year of use. Protection lasts for five years, and can be renewed for another five years. Before applying for registration, it's prudent to conduct a preliminary search to confirm that the design does not conflict with other registered designs. Once approved, as with other types of intellectual property, industrial designs can be sold or licensed to third parties, in which case the licensees should be registered with the Industrial Design Office.

This brief survey barely covers these very complex issues. If a distinct trade mark, a unique product or an industrial design are important parts of your competitive edge, you should take steps to protect that edge. While you can do the work yourself, it's advisable to retain a trade mark or patent agent, or a lawyer who specializes in intellectual property. If your application is poorly drafted, you may not be protected. "Intellectual property is one of the most complex areas of the law," Dobbin notes. "You should really look for someone with experience in that area."

PARTNERSHIP AND SHAREHOLDER AGREEMENTS

When a business begins, the partners are naturally optimistic. Even so, the possibility of a dispute and dissolution should be addressed in the partnership or shareholders' agreement. "You've got to assume that something might go wrong," Dobbin explains. "People often think that's unnecessary, and see agreements as an unnecessary expense. But people do fall out. You should provide an efficient way of handling that, one that maintains the value of people's investment in the business. The agreement should also stipulate the responsibilities of the partners, and their respective contributions. Who can make capital expenditures? Who can call for loans?"

The cost of cutting corners can be very high, says Levitan. Shareholders and partnership disputes are a major cause of legal problems for owner/managers, he notes. Nonetheless, many entrepreneurs try to cut corners here. The agreement might be drafted by one partner's lawyer. But there's a risk that it could be weighted in that partner's favour, he cautions. An incompetently drafted agreement can create a deadlock in the event of a dispute. "They expect to be able to extricate themselves, but end up paying $50,000 to $60,000 in litigation fees. If they had spent $2,000 or $3,000 in the first place, they wouldn't be in that mess. It happens every day."

OTHER CONTRACTS

Dobbin says the same corner-cutting goes on with complex contracts. "People sign contracts without getting legal advice," he observes. "They'll come in with an executed document and ask what the lawyer may think." People should always be aware of what they're signing, and sometimes it takes a lawyer to tell them. If they don't know what's in the agreement, they forgo the opportunity to negotiate.

As we saw in Chapter 5, leases can contain a variety of charges. Under participating leases, the tenant pays the landlord a percentage of gross in addition to the basic rent. Under net-net leases, landlords pass on the costs of operating the facility to tenants. "I've had many clients come two months after signing a lease, thinking their rent would be $3,000 plus a small percentage. Then they get whacked with a bill for $33,000 as their share in property taxes," Levitan relates.

"Particularly with complex leases, you need a good lawyer or accountant to determine your exposure."

FRANCHISE AGREEMENTS

As we discussed in Chapter 2, franchisees should consider what they're getting for their money, and what they're paying before signing a franchise agreement. "Are you just getting the use of a name?" Dobbin asks. "Or are you getting training, manuals, a site or assistance in locating a site? What are you paying? What's the real bottom line? Are there charges for supplies, management, advertising? Sometimes there's real misunderstanding about what the franchisor does and does not offer."

LOAN AGREEMENTS

Before signing a loan agreement, you should consider what kind of commitment you're getting from the lender, and what you're giving up in terms of interest and security. "Be careful that you don't give everything away in case you need further financing," Dobbin advises. "The amount of security may be negotiable if you have a track record."

It's prudent to have a qualified lawyer examine any important document before you sign. But a business starting on a shoestring may not be able to afford to have its lawyer look over every single document, Levitan realizes. If you've read the document and think you understand it, and you want to sign without incurring the expense of having your lawyer review it, he suggests you draft a business letter outlining your understanding of the agreement, and have the other party sign it. If the legal document doesn't conform with the letter, the letter may prove useful in the event of a dispute.

SELECTING A LAWYER

As the foregoing discussion demonstrates, the law is very complex. There are lawyers specializing in tax, in real estate, in labour relations, in corporate/commercial law, in intellectual property, in litigation. "It's a mistake to have one person deal with everything," Levitan maintains. "The law has become very specialized. A simple real estate deal might have very serious tax consequences. You need to use specialists." It's not uncommon to have a general lawyer to look after routine legal matters, then retain a specialist when specific needs arise. As with accountants, one possibility is to deal with a medium to large firm that can supply a variety of services. "You have everything under one roof," Levitan explains, "but the firm might not be as strong in one area as others."

As an alternative, Levitan suggests you inform yourself about your legal needs, and then find a lawyer, or lawyers, who can best address them. You also find lawyers in the Yellow Pages, through advertisements or through referral services operated by the law societies that govern legal practice in each province. One of the best ways, Levitan says, is just to ask around. If you're facing a specific legal issue, ask for referrals from other businesses that have faced similar issues. "A few names will keep cropping up," he says.

Businesses in smaller centres won't have as many options. But Levitan says small-town lawyers usually know their limits. "You can trust the global judgment of a small-town lawyer more than one in a major centre. In cities, lawyers are directed into specialties and tend to lose touch with other areas. Small-town lawyers usually practise in all areas." But you should be sure the lawyer will call a specialist if he or she doesn't know the answer to a question.

As with any professional, you should prepare in advance for the initial meeting with a lawyer. "If there's a specific problem, it's always good to put a chronological outline of the events on paper," Levitan suggests. "That will save a lot of time and money. And be very frank. Nothing annoys a lawyer more than finding out after that a client didn't tell the truth."

If you're looking for help with a specific problem, you want to assess the lawyer's expertise in that area. "If the lawyer gives general rather than specific answers," Levitan says, "that's a sign that he or she doesn't have expertise in that area." If you're looking for a general lawyer, you'll be relying on gut feel as much as hard fact. Explains Levitan: "It boils down to trust. Do you feel confident about that person's judgment?"

Costs

Usually, legal services are billed on an hourly basis. You can be billed for all time spent in your service, including telephone calls, meetings, research, preparing documents and correspondence, time in court, and so on. In addition to services rendered, you'll have to pay disbursements, that is, out-of-pocket expenses incurred by your lawyer for things like photocopies and couriers. In some provinces, lawyers can work on contingency fee basis. Instead of an hourly rate, they agree to accept a percentage of the money collected on your behalf, plus disbursements. For some services where time requirements are predictable, the lawyer may be willing to work for a flat fee.

Sometimes you'll have to pay a retainer, essentially a pre-payment for services rendered. The retainer is kept in a trust account, and money released to the lawyer as services are rendered.

Costs should be addressed at the initial meeting. Cautions Levitan: "If a lawyer avoids the question of fees, or deals with it vaguely; if he's not prepared to state an hourly rate and an anticipated fee, that's usually a sign that you might not want to use him."

If you believe you've been overcharged for legal services and your lawyer won't adjust your bill, you can take the bill to an assessment officer associated with the court. The lawyer will be asked to justify the invoice. "More often than not, the bill isn't just reduced, it's *slashed*," says Levitan. "If you want to continue relations with that lawyer," he adds, "it's best to work it out privately."

The same rules that govern relations with other professional advisers apply to lawyers. More than most business relationships, the lawyer-client relationship requires trust and confidence. You'll be relying on your lawyer to help you prevent legal problems, and to help you deal with problems that almost inevitably occur in any business.

11/The Big-Ticket Items:
Justifying, Purchasing and Implementing Fixed Assets

When Zepf Technologies Inc. started in 1972, it was a low-tech garage operation. Then, in 1978, the Waterloo, Ontario, firm purchased $750,000 worth of computerized numerical control (CNC) factory machinery to automate manufacture of its products. In 1982, it spent another $1.2 million on computer-aided design (CAD) equipment to streamline product design and development.

Zepf Technologies manufactures transfer systems for containers. Using its systems, a customer could blow a shampoo bottle from plastic, fill the bottle, label it and screw on the top. CEO Larry Zepf estimates that 50 percent of his fiscal 1989 sales of $4.5 million are a result of the modernization. The new equipment has permitted him to address new markets that otherwise would have been inaccessible. In addition, Zepf Technologies' high-tech image impresses customers. "We use high-tech as a marketing tool. Our customers know we're committed to this business. It takes away their concerns about service."

With the CAD system, engineers can design new products, using information from previous designs. The system can run animations to show how the products will fit into customers' factories. Once a design is complete, it's sent to CNC equipment for post-processing. Numerical-controlled equipment such as lathes, mills and cam-cutting machines produce goods automatically based on information from the CAD system. Prior to buying the CNC equipment, half of the products were made by skilled workers using hand-operated machines. But half couldn't be made at all. In addition, products are manufactured more accurately and more quickly, with less-skilled operators.

Still, things didn't work out as well as they might have, Zepf acknowledges. With one of the CNC machines, his company was able to create products for a niche market where it's the only supplier. The other machine produces goods for a crowded market. "There, we're just another boy on the block," he says. Since purchasing the CNC equipment, the company has doubled its sales. But Zepf believes sales could have quadrupled had both machines enabled him to attack lucrative niche markets.

The CAD system hasn't done everything the company had hoped it would do, and enhancements to the CAD programs provided by the software vendor have had glitches. But Zepf doesn't regret buying the system. The company spent two years deciding which system to get; the one they selected was the best available at the time. If Zepf had it to do over again, however, he wouldn't have equipped all of his engineers with CAD. He's spent $400,000 on CAD software over the last five years. He figures he could have saved half of that.

VITAL DECISIONS

Zepf Technologies' fixed-asset purchases profoundly influenced its direction. Despite the flaws noted by Zepf, his decisions worked out well, enabling him to pursue new markets.

Fixed assets are items of enduring value purchased by a firm in the expectation of future benefits. A firm purchasing a truck so it can handle its own shipping, thereby cutting transportation costs, is making a fixed-asset decision. So is a restaurant adding seating capacity so it can increase sales. As Zepf Technologies did, a company might acquire fixed assets so that it can offer new products. Or it might purchase assets that enable it to increase its capacity to make current products.

Many business decisions have risks attached. But fixed-asset decisions are critical. They often involve a large outlay of cash. Often, assets are paid for over a long period. And for many assets, such as specialized factory machinery, there's no second-hand market. Businesses usually have to live with their decisions for a long time. These decisions can affect a firm's direction years after they're made.

RISKS

How well a firm handles purchases of fixed assets can determine its survival. Suppose, for example, that there was no market for the products made by Zepf's equipment, or that the markets for these products were extremely competitive. The revenue produced by the equipment would be insufficient to offset its cost. What if the equipment turned out to be unreliable? Maintenance costs might increase, and the firm might be unable to deliver on time. What if the equipment was inappropriate for Zepf's operation? The company might be stuck with useless, expensive machinery, or might face high expenses in trying to adapt the equipment to its operation, or the operation to the equipment. What if it was rendered obsolete by more advanced equipment soon after it was purchased? If competitors purchased cheaper, more capable equipment, they'd have a significant edge.

Zepf minimized these risks by carefully selecting his equipment. But he acknowledges that deciding to purchase the equipment in the first place was based more on "gut feel" than on solid analysis. That's a mistake many companies make. As a result, they may invest in assets that produce little return. Or they may purchase equipment inappropriate for the purpose. The risk is greatest if the company has little experience with the type of asset being purchased.

ISSUES

Selection criteria vary widely among different asset types. That's why experience in purchasing specific assets can be so important. For a truck, operating costs, reliability, serviceability and resale value are important issues. With computers, reliability and serviceability are certainly factors. But because most people use them till they're obsolete, resale isn't an issue at all.

Still, fixed-asset purchases can be broken down into five steps. The first is justification, determining whether the asset has genuine payback potential. The second is selection, choosing a specific product. The third is the purchase itself, choosing a supplier and agreeing to terms. The fourth is implementation, making the asset work for the business. The final stage is review, making sure the asset is benefiting the business.

JUSTIFICATION

Justifying asset purchases involves comparing the cost of the asset with the benefits derived from it. You start by determining the probable increases in income, or decreases in expenses, the asset will generate. From this you subtract operating costs associated with the asset. A restaurant adding extra capacity might have to consider extra rent and salaries for servers to look after the area, for example. The net benefit is compared with the cost of acquiring the asset.

Cost-justification is important for several reasons. First of all, it tells you whether the asset is actually a good investment, whether it will make money for the business. Second, a thorough justification will make it much easier for the business to obtain financing for the asset, if that's necessary. Finally, most businesses have limited financial resources. A thorough analysis will help them choose the most lucrative assets for purchase.

Cost-justification is done implicitly by most buyers, but few buyers analyse the purchase formally. Indeed, cost-justification isn't necessary for every asset purchase. It doesn't make a lot of sense to cost-justify a $300 typewriter, for example. Not only is it a relatively inexpensive asset, its function in the business isn't critical. Capital acquisitions such as Zepf's, however, are critical for their cost and for their vital function.

If a company does any kind of formal analysis at all, it usually involves determining an asset's payback period or the asset's rate of return. While these two forms of analysis are better than none at all, they ignore basic business issues. The first fundamental rule of acquisition is, the greater the income produced by your assets, the better. Second, it's better if income is produced sooner rather than later. Third, it's better if expenses are incurred later rather than sooner.

PAYBACK ANALYSIS
Payback analysis involves determining the length of time it will take to recover the cost of an asset, and comparing that against a theoretical standard. This method has two weaknesses. First, it doesn't show whether one asset purchase will produce more income than another. Two assets of the same cost might have the same payback period, but one might produce income for a far longer period than another. The second asset would be a more favourable investment for the company, but payback-period analysis alone wouldn't show this. Of two assets with the same payback period, one might produce income earlier than the other. Again, payback analysis wouldn't show this.

RATE OF RETURN
Rate-of-return analysis shows how much income an asset can produce over its life, and so is preferable to simple payback analysis.

To determine rate of return, you determine the net income the asset produces in each year. From gross income, you subtract operating expenses associated with the asset, and depreciation of the asset. Next, you determine the average income over the life of the asset. The next step is to determine the book value of the asset in each year. In year one, you subtract depreciation from the price of the asset. In the second and subsequent years, you subtract depreciation from the depreciated value at the end of the previous year. Next, determine the average book value over the life of the asset. Divide average income by average value, and you have the rate of return.

These methods will show whether one asset will produce more income than another, but it won't show how quickly it will produce that income.

DISCOUNTED CASHFLOW

To evaluate fixed-asset purchases properly, you need a method that takes into account the fact that a dollar of income earned today is more valuable than one earned next year or five years from now. Assets don't always produce income evenly. It may take several months to get new machinery up and running, and to get workers trained to use it. Because of this lead time and initial expenses, the equipment may not produce an income in the first year. Each of Zepf's 10 engineers spent 3 months learning to use the CAD system after it was installed, a requirement that obviously affected its contribution to profit in year one.

To use this method, you determine the net present value of the asset. That sounds more complex than it really is. What you're doing is determining how much each dollar of future income is worth to you today, and comparing that with the cost of the asset.

DIFFERENT POSSIBILITIES

To start with, you have to determine the income the asset will produce, again net of operating expenses, for each year of its life. That may be difficult. If you're not sure how much income the asset will produce in any given year, work out alternative scenarios, and assign a probability to each. You might, for example, decide that there's a 25 percent chance the asset will produce income of $100,000; a 50 percent chance it will produce $150,000 and a 25 percent chance it will produce $180,000. You can have as many scenarios as you like, but the probabilities must add up to 100 percent. For each scenario, multiply the projected income by the probability. Adding the results will give you the probable incremental income for that year.

	Income	Probability	Result
Scenario 1	$100,000	25%	$25,000
Scenario 2	150,000	50%	75,000
Scenario 3	180,000	25%	75,000
Projected Incremental Income			$145,000

If you're unsure of operating expenses, you can use the same method to work out an average result for different expense scenarios.

INCOME TAX

Since you're trying to determine the cash income the asset will produce, you have to consider the taxman's bite on your profits. You're allowed to deduct interest and depreciation from income, so you can deduct these costs from the net incremental income produced by the asset for the purposes of determining the tax you'll have to pay on the extra profit the asset will produce. Since these are real expenses, you have to add them in later.

THE FORMULA

If you don't have a head for numbers, this sounds more complex than it really is. What you're actually doing is a projected profit-and-loss statement, not for your entire company, but just for the asset in question. Let's look at what we've got so far. You start by determining the income produced by the asset during each year of its life, and deducting expenses, such as increased salaries or rent, associated with the asset. If you're not sure of expenses, average out different scenarios, using the method described above. Subtract projected incremental expenses from projected incremental income, and you have the benefit produced by the asset. Subtract interest and depreciation, and you have the net benefit before income tax. Multiply the net benefit by your income-tax rate to determine the tax you'll pay on the extra income produced by the asset. Subtract that from net income before tax to determine net income after tax. You'll have to add depreciation and interest back in to determine the cash income from the asset for each year, because you'll deal with these expenses when you calculate the net present value of the asset.

Repeat the exercise for every year you expect to own the asset. For the last year, add the trade-in or resale value of the asset, if any, to the cash income for that year.

DISCOUNT RATES

The next step is to determine the present value of this future income. First, add the interest you'll have to pay to finance the acquisition (or the interest income you'd forgo if you're paying cash) to your profit objective. If you're paying 13 percent interest to finance the acquisition, and your profit objective is 5 percent, then the discount rate for determining the present value of future income is 18 percent. Next, use that rate and a present value table (it works just like an interest table, but in reverse) to calculate the present value of income in each year of ownership. (Many financial calculators and personal computer financial modelling programs will do present value calculations.)

On the table produced on page 172, successive years of ownership are arrayed in vertical columns, increasing discount rates in horizontal rows. For a discount rate of 18 percent, the factors for years one through five are 0.847, 0.718, 0.609, 0.516 and 0.437. To determine the present value of income produced by the assets in years one through five for a company with after-tax profit objective of 5 percent paying 13 percent to finance the asset, you'd multiply the cash income in each year by those factors. For this hypothetical company, incremental income of $10,000 in year one is worth $8,470 today. Incremental income of $10,000 in years two through five is presently worth $7,180, $6,090, $5,160 and $4,370. Total the present value of the income produced by the asset in each year. Subtract total present value of future income from the initial cost of the asset, and you have the net present value of the asset to the company. The higher the net present value, the better the investment. If the net present value is negative, the asset is a poor investment.

WEIGHING ALTERNATIVES

Few firms have all the management and financial resources required to explore every opportunity available to them. Would it be better to enlarge a present location, or open a branch in another town? The net-present-value method can also be used to compare different courses of action.

You can use discounted cashflows to evaluate competing fixed-asset proposals. Should you buy less expensive machinery that

YEAR	1%	2%	3%	4%	5%	6%	7%	8%	9%	10%	12%	14%	15%	16%	18%	20%	24%
1	.990	.980	.971	.962	.952	.943	.935	.926	.917	.909	.893	.877	.870	.862	.847	.833	.806
2	.980	.961	.943	.925	.907	.890	.873	.857	.842	.826	.797	.769	.756	.743	.718	.694	.650
3	.971	.942	.915	.889	.864	.840	.816	.794	.772	.751	.712	.675	.658	.641	.609	.579	.524
4	.961	.924	.889	.855	.823	.792	.763	.735	.708	.683	.636	.592	.572	.552	.516	.482	.423
5	.951	.906	.863	.822	.784	.747	.713	.681	.650	.621	.567	.519	.497	.476	.437	.402	.341
6	.942	.888	.838	.790	.746	.705	.666	.630	.596	.564	.507	.456	.432	.410	.370	.335	.275
7	.933	.871	.813	.760	.711	.665	.623	.583	.547	.513	.452	.400	.376	.354	.314	.279	.222
8	.923	.853	.789	.731	.677	.627	.582	.540	.502	.467	.404	.351	.327	.305	.266	.233	.179
9	.914	.837	.766	.703	.645	.592	.544	.500	.460	.424	.361	.308	.284	.263	.226	.194	.144
10	.905	.820	.744	.676	.614	.558	.508	.463	.422	.386	.322	.270	.247	.227	.191	.162	.116
11	.896	.804	.722	.650	.585	.527	.475	.429	.388	.350	.287	.237	.215	.195	.162	.135	.094
12	.887	.788	.701	.625	.557	.497	.444	.397	.356	.319	.257	.208	.187	.168	.137	.112	.076
13	.879	.773	.681	.601	.530	.469	.415	.368	.326	.290	.229	.182	.163	.145	.116	.093	.061
14	.870	.758	.661	.577	.505	.442	.388	.340	.299	.263	.205	.160	.141	.125	.099	.078	.049
15	.861	.743	.642	.555	.481	.417	.362	.315	.275	.239	.183	.140	.123	.108	.084	.065	.040
16	.853	.728	.623	.534	.458	.394	.339	.292	.252	.218	.163	.123	.107	.093	.071	.054	.032
17	.844	.714	.605	.513	.436	.371	.317	.270	.231	.198	.146	.108	.093	.080	.060	.045	.026
18	.836	.700	.587	.494	.416	.350	.296	.250	.212	.180	.130	.095	.081	.069	.051	.038	.021
19	.828	.686	.570	.475	.396	.331	.276	.232	.194	.164	.116	.083	.070	.060	.043	.031	.017
20	.820	.673	.554	.456	.377	.319	.258	.215	.178	.149	.104	.073	.061	.051	.037	.026	.014
25	.780	.610	.478	.375	.295	.233	.184	.146	.116	.092	.059	.038	.030	.024	.016	.010	.005
30	.742	.552	.412	.308	.231	.174	.131	.099	.075	.057	.033	.020	.015	.012	.007	.004	.002

you'll outgrow in a few years or more expensive equipment that will last you several years? Perhaps the less expensive equipment also has lower operating costs. And with developing technology it may be less expensive to upgrade later. However, you might have to pay installation costs twice. And the more expensive machine may enable you to increase volumes quickly should such an opportunity arise. Determining the net present value of the two alternatives will help you make a decision.

You can also use this method to compare the relative advantages of leasing and purchasing. When projecting the future income produced by a leased asset, you'd include the lease payments with operating expenses associated with the asset, rather than factoring in depreciation and interest. Having determined future income and worked out its present value, you'd subtract the initial cost of the asset, which, because it's leased, is nil. Compare that with the net present value of the asset under a purchase scenario to determine the best course of action.

Predictions for future income will probably involve as much gut feel as hard fact. The advantage of using discounted cashflows to evaluate fixed-asset purchase possibilities is that it takes into account basic business principles ignored by less rigorous cost-justification methods. And it forces you to consider different possibilities. This method won't eliminate guesswork. But it should minimize it.

BUYING FOR THE RIGHT REASONS

Any business has limited funds to invest in new assets, so it's vital to invest in areas that will produce the greatest return. Almost always, you'll get a greater return if you focus on increasing revenue rather than reducing costs. A computerized accounting system, for example, can reduce bookkeeping costs. But by using it to analyse sales patterns, a business can increase its revenues.

That's what happened with O'Donals Family Restaurants of Victoria, B.C. The company wanted to expand, but was concerned about control of cash and inventory at remote locations. So it looked into computer systems that would give it that control. "We're a cashflow business," says president Don Michaels. "We have to control our money, and we need to know what's selling. Before we were just guessing."

LOWER COSTS

The computers gave O'Donals that control. They've been installed in the company's five restaurants at a cost of $25,000 per location. Now servers enter orders by touching the appropriate areas of computer screens installed in the serving areas. Orders are then printed out on printers located in the kitchen. Food won't be cooked until an order has been entered onto the computer; and once it's entered, it has to be paid for unless the manager deletes it. This eliminates the possibility of servers giving freebies to friends.

As it turned out, that's the least of the system's benefits. With the system, servers are more efficient. "Servers never have to go back to the kitchen, except to pick up orders," Michaels explains. "We can get by with one less server per shift." Such errors as preparing the wrong kind of food have been eliminated. Those errors used to cost the company tens of thousands of dollars per year. Food spoilage has also been reduced.

HIGHER SALES

But the big benefits have been with revenue enhancement. The system produces reports showing slow- and fast-selling items. "When we do a menu review, we always delete one item if we add an item. With information from the computer, we know we're selling people what they want to buy."

The computer also shows Michaels which servers are performing best. If someone's not selling desserts, he or she can be told about the importance of suggestion selling for the restaurant's income and his or her own.

SELECTION

Before you can select a specific product, you have to determine what exactly you expect the asset to do for your business, and what product features you'll require. For some kinds of assets, sales people's cars, for example, selection criteria are straightforward. For other products, they're much more complex. Businesses buy too many kinds of assets to make any useful generalizations. As observed above, selection criteria for a truck and a computer are quite different.

To select the right product, you have to know what these selection criteria are. What should you look for in a truck or in a computer? What will make one kind of truck or computer suitable for a business, and another kind unsuitable? To get the right answers, you have to know what kinds of questions you should ask. To know the right questions, you have to have an idea of what's available.

EXPERTISE

With most assets, companies will want to consider purchase cost, operating costs, reliability, serviceability and resale potential. But the most difficult issue to address is the most important one: which product will best perform the task I have in mind?

If the asset is going to have a significant impact on either your balance sheet or your profit-and-loss statement, it's critical that you know what you're doing. You can rely on the people selling the asset for information, or you can try to learn the field yourself. But if you're inexperienced with the kind of asset you're buying, there's a real risk you might make a poor decision. And as we've seen, poor fixed-asset decisions can be very costly. Retaining a consultant familiar with the asset in question will reduce the possibility of a poor decision.

PURCHASE

Once you've determined which product to buy, you have to decide on a supplier and purchase terms. Particularly if you're an inexperienced buyer, the selection of the supplier can be as important as the selection of the asset. That's especially true if getting the asset up and running is going to be a challenge, or if you're going to be relying on the vendor for after-sale service and support. Conversely, you might consider a less expensive, less service-oriented supplier if you have experience with that type of asset.

GUARANTEES

Sometimes it's not possible to buy from a premium supplier. The appropriate product may be available only from a second-tier supplier. In any case, guarantees for service and support should be negotiated as part of the acquisition contract. If the asset is being implemented over a period of time, you should specify holdbacks with respect to performance. Holdbacks are common in the construction industry. Contractors are usually paid in phases as they complete specified portions of the job. Similarly, milestone payments might be negotiated as part of a contract with a company providing specialized computer software. Under such a contract, payment would be given after specified portions of the program were successfully installed. Specific requirements for asset features or performance should also be included as part of the contract.

Decisions about fixed assets are among the most important a company will ever make. For that reason, professional advisers should be involved at every stage. If the asset is significant for the health of the business, you should get advice from your lawyer about the acquisition contract. Input from your accountant and banker about the financial aspects of the acquisition is also advisable.

IMPLEMENTATION

If the asset is being implemented over time, one person should be made responsible for successful implementation. That person will be responsible for making all the arrangements necessary for installation of the asset, such as training, space, utilities and so on. A schedule for implementation, outlining the key milestones, should be drawn up. If a company doesn't appoint someone to oversee implementation, it can take two to four times longer to get the asset up and running. Consider paying a bonus if implementation is completed on time and on budget.

THE HUMAN SIDE

Companies should be aware that installing new technology can cause serious personnel problems. New technology often changes the way people work in a business; and employees may resist these changes. To address their fears, companies might inform employees of impending change, and get their input. They may have valuable ideas about how the change should be handled; at the very least, involving them beforehand will help allay their fears.

Companies should also make sure employees are properly trained to use the asset. With some assets, such as sales people's cars, no training is necessary. All management has to do is determine that the car is actually being used. But if the asset is foreign to the company, if new technology is being introduced, the company will have to provide training if it wants to get the most out of the asset. Often, companies give employees a manual and expect them to learn on their own. That's ineffective. If they learn to use the asset at all, they'll learn slowly. In extreme cases, they may even quit. Instead, employees should be *shown* how to use the asset. Proper training helps the company use the asset productively more quickly. It reduces the disruption that inevitably occurs when new technology is introduced.

O'Donals Restaurants' computer supplier provided each server with two hours of training in the restaurants. Managers went outside for training. Even so, Michaels says, some people had trouble during the first few days. "One waitress – a university student – was crying because she couldn't cope with the system," he recalls. "But then she got onto it. We were concerned about one individual – our oldest employee – but she caught on right away, and now trains new employees to use the system. With all our people, once they catch on there's no problem."

PERFORMANCE REVIEW

Work doesn't stop once the asset is justified, purchased and installed. After it's implemented, management should review the asset's performance. Is it producing the extra income that was expected originally? Are operating costs in line with projections? If not, management should determine the reasons for the variance, and take corrective action. People may not be using the equipment properly, and may need supplemental training. There may be organizational barriers blocking productive use of the asset. For example, management may not be acting on the reports generated by a computer. Making assets work productively requires a commitment from management.

For O'Donals Family Restaurants, using their computer system productively meant finding out who their best servers were, and encouraging poor performers to do better. As we've seen, the company also uses computer reports when it's making menu changes. "We're taking reports from our computer and acting on them," says Michaels.

12/Managing Crisis:
What to Do When Trouble Strikes

The new product Bill Mulock introduced in 1986 was so successful it almost killed his company. His father, a 29-year veteran of Swifts Canada, had started Tasty Chip Steak Products Ltd. 28 years earlier as a supplier of high-quality peameal bacon. The Toronto firm's clients include major food chains and food service companies, who in turn sell to restaurants.

Loblaws, the grocery chain, approached Mulock in March 1986 about supplying packaged peameal bacon for retail sale. By that time, Tasty Chip Steak Products had 75 percent of the Ontario market for bulk peameal bacon. No one had ever offered packaged peameal bacon. Peameal bacon is wet after it's processed; for the package to seal, the meat has to be dry. However, packaging technology was changing quickly; and Mulock decided to grasp this opportunity. In November of that year, the first packaged product came off his line.

"It sold like crazy," Mulock recalls. Each of five major chains was ordering 175 cases a day. But Mulock wasn't aware that the more bacon he sold, the more money he lost. Because Tasty Chip Steak's bulk-packaged bacon was so profitable, the losses didn't show up for almost a year. But as sales of packaged product grew, so did the firm's losses, which ultimately became "severely threatening." Its year-end review in August 1987 made the problem obvious. Its bank line had steadily increased, and the bank had become alarmed. Rather than see the company die, Mulock says, "We decided to grab the bull by the horns and solve the problem."

His first step was to learn everything he could about cost analysis from his accountant. He installed a computerized accounting system so he could monitor costs on a monthly basis. Then Mulock applied what he had learned to his company. As it turned out, the problem was simple. "The product wasn't priced high enough." To begin with, Mulock had spent $180,000 on new machinery, and hadn't factored that cost into the price. And to satisfy demand for his packaged bacon, he had to pay overtime, which he didn't account for in pricing.

To reduce overtime, Mulock spent $85,000 on a deluxe meat-slicer that does the work of four standard machines. That let him take six people off the line. Next, he contacted his customers, and explained why he had to raise prices 12 to 14 percent. "They all told me to charge what I had to," Mulock remembers. Ironically, he could have charged more all along, being the sole supplier of packaged peameal bacon. But he was accustomed to the competitive meat-packing industry, where net profits are typically 1 percent, and was worried that customers might not buy the product if it were priced too high.

To make his plan work, Mulock needed the co-operation of his bank. Seeing that all his equipment was paid for, it was willing to give him time to turn the business around. "The bank kept our doors open and honoured our cheques, but insisted on controls," Mulock recalls. The account manager increased Mulock's line of credit, but required personal guarantees backed by Mulock's own assets, something he had not had to provide for years. "I had no problem with that," he says. "I'm mad that it happened, but I understand the bank's position. Banks don't operate out of the goodness of their hearts. They're unemotional—as they should be."

After accumulating losses of $250,000, Tasty Chip Steak Products showed a modest profit in December 1988. And with U.S. markets opening for its packaged product, the future looks rosy. Once the company's been profitable for a year, Mulock plans to ask the bank to give him back his guarantees, and anticipates a positive response.

He's blunt about the source of his company's problems. "It was management. It was me. We probably needed a good shot to wake us up." The shot woke him up to other problems, and other opportunities. Cost analysis showed he was paying far too much for some replacement parts. The U.S.-based supplier of one piece of machinery was charging $146 for a bearing. For warranty protection, original parts were required. Mulock decided to forgo the warranty and buy bearings locally. The price: $9 each.

He now carries a non-competing Quebec packer's products along with his own in his trucks, a deal that allowed the Quebec company to enter the Ontario market. Payments for the service have bought Tasty Chip Steak Products a new $55,000 truck and cover the salaries of three drivers, two loading dock staff and a foreman. What was once an expense has become a profit centre.

The specifics of Tasty Chip Steak Products' problems may be unique to the company. The general pattern isn't, nor is the solution. There aren't many businesses that have been around for very long that have *never* faced some kind of crisis. However, not all of them weather the storm.

CRISIS AVOIDANCE

Those that do have some things in common. First, management accepts responsibility, and looks at the mistakes that brought on the crisis. What was the problem? Uncontrolled spending on unnecessary expenses? Excessive capital investment? Excessive inventory or inventory that doesn't move? Lower-than-anticipated sales? Uncompetitive products or prices? Failure to collect receivables caused by excessively liberal credit policies? Perhaps the operator has failed to attend to a critical part of the business, such as accounting or marketing, or perhaps he or she lacks expertise in some critical area. Perhaps personal problems have led the owner/manager to neglect the business.

Factors beyond the owner's control can also induce a crisis. But it's the role of management to anticipate changes and adjust for them, notes Joe Miller, vice-president and Ontario regional general manager for the Federal Business Development Bank. If the market for a company's product softens, why didn't management shift to other products before crisis set in? If the economy softens and interest rates rise, why didn't management take steps to pare inventories and expenses? If a key customer goes bankrupt, why were the firm's fortunes tied so closely to a single customer, and why did the firm continue to extend credit? If a key employee leaves the firm, why didn't management keep him or her tied with a more attractive compensation package or involve the employee in ownership, or why didn't it train someone else to take his or her place? We can elaborate on this theme *ad infinitum*. The bottom line is this: the best form of crisis management is crisis avoidance.

The fact is that most crises are avoidable, Miller maintains.

"Sometimes problems grow into crises because management doesn't have the right information. If you're getting monthly information, you can see problems before they become crises. If you can anticipate a crisis, you can develop a plan." One element of crisis avoidance is, thus, timely information, and the willingness to act on it. As we've seen, that's one of the lessons Mulock learned from his experience. Similarly, owner/managers have to be aware of external factors that could affect their businesses.

Most of the time, firms do avoid crisis, not through any single dramatic act, but through competent day-to-day management. However, in business as in baseball, no one bats 1.000. You can foresee some problems, but not every problem.

CRISIS MANAGEMENT

Too many companies avoid confronting their problems, says Gar Pynn, director of the P.J. Gardiner Institute for Small Business Studies at Memorial University in St. John's, Newfoundland. "Often they wait till the bailiff's at the door to confront their problems. They may have cashflow problems and not know why. They edge up over their bank lines, and the manager pulls the plug. If they knew what was going on, they could go to their bank managers with the information. Perhaps their sales are up and they need more money to finance increased inventory."

Whatever the problem, you're going to need others' help in addressing it. They include bankers, trade creditors, your accountant and, if appropriate, customers. Don't avoid them. One reason Mulock was able to save his company was that he worked with his bank and customers to correct his problems.

"Bankers don't want surprises," notes Gerry LeJan, manager of the Royal Bank's independent business centre in downtown Toronto. "What concerns us the most is when all of a sudden a client starts bouncing cheques. If we know there's a problem, we can help find a solution. If we don't, we can't offer any kind of help. We rely heavily on the integrity of our clients. If we feel we're not being fairly treated, it can taint the whole relationship once trust is breached."

QUICK FIXES ...
Too often, businesses attempt quick fixes to their problems, LeJan

comments. They might dump product below cost to meet a bank payment. Of course, this just delays the day of reckoning and worsens the business's situation. "If we're informed of the situation, we'll tell the client not to overreact. Quick fixes aren't the solution. Our goal is to develop long-lasting relationships. If we can maintain our relationship, that's in the best interest of both parties."

Like any problem, a business problem can seem worse than it really is. Avoiding it makes it seem worse. Notes LeJan: "The client may perceive as major a problem that, in the bank's eyes, happens regularly. Or other clients in the same industry may be having the same problem. We may be able to suggest measures that others in the same position have taken.

... AND REAL SOLUTIONS

"The first two people you should phone when you have a problem are your banker and your accountant," he advises. "At first, you can just let the bank know you're having a problem. Then work out a plan with your accountant." The bank wants to know four things: the nature of the problem; how it happened; how you plan to address it; and what you want from the bank. If the plan is sound, the bank might be able to advance more money, suspend repayment or adjust the advance rate on receivables and inventory. Of course, as happened with Mulock, you may have to offer additional security to the bank to take into account the greater risk.

Hidden in almost any crisis is an opportunity. Often owner/managers emerge from crises stronger than ever; almost always they emerge wiser. The history of Tasty Chip Steak Products bears that out.

Sometimes owner/managers can work out of a crisis with their accountants and bankers. Sometimes they need outside help. As we saw in Chapter 6, John Cameron brought in a consultant to help him deal with his window-installation company's crisis.

BANKRUPTCY

Sometimes the situation is so serious that the business cannot meet all its debts. To stay alive, it needs to work out a solution with creditors. And sometimes it's just not possible to keep the company afloat. In these cases, advice from your accountant and lawyer is essential.

THE BANKRUPTCY PROCESS

There are three ways a business or individual can become bankrupt. An insolvent person or corporation may voluntarily place itself in bankruptcy. If it makes a debt-restructuring proposal under the Bankruptcy Act that is not accepted by its creditors or the court, it will be placed in bankruptcy. Finally, it can be petitioned into involuntary bankruptcy by an unsecured creditor providing the debt owed to the creditor is $1,000 or more and the debtor has committed one of 10 "acts of bankruptcy" as defined in the Bankruptcy Act.

The most common act of bankruptcy is failing to meet liabilities as they become due. Others include notifying creditors that it is suspending payment of the debt, attempting to evade the debt by leaving the country, and disposing of assets with intent to defraud the creditors.

Debtors can contest a petition for bankruptcy. But once the court has adjudged a debtor to be bankrupt, or once a debtor files an assignment in bankruptcy, the process is more or less similar. A licensed trustee takes control of the bankrupt's property, calls a meeting of creditors at which inspectors are appointed to guide the trustee. Ultimately, the trustee disposes of the firm's assets, and distributes the proceeds to creditors.

To do that, he or she obtains the bankrupt's financial records and other pertinent documents, including a full list of the bankrupt firm's (or person's) assets and liabilities, with names and addresses of all creditors.

The trustee must confirm that assets have not been improperly disposed of, say through sale at low prices to friends or relatives; and that the bankrupt has not been more favourable to some of its creditors than to others. Creditors are instructed to file proofs of claim that set out the debt to them. Once a corporation or person is bankrupt, unsecured creditors cannot sue to collect debts from the bankrupt. In some instances, they can ask the court for permission to commence legal action against the bankrupt.

After all assets and debts are accounted for, the trustee disposes of assets in such a way as to obtain the highest possible return for creditors. That may entail selling assets piecemeal, say by auction, or by selling the assets entire, so that the buyer can resume operation of the business.

THE PECKING ORDER

Like a pride of lions devouring a carcase, creditors observe a strict hierarchy when dividing the remains of a bankrupt company. First pickings go to *secured creditors*, that is, creditors who hold mortgages, chattel mortgages or other forms of security on specific company assets or all its assets. Next come *preferred creditors*, including the trustee (who can collect fees and disbursements), landlords (who can collect three months' back rent and three months' accelerated rent), government and employees (who can collect a limited amount of back wages and vacation pay). In some provinces, priorities have been juggled so that some debt owing to government, such as the employee portion of withholding tax, takes priority over secured creditors. If there are any proceeds from the realization of assets remaining after secured and preferred creditors, these are distributed to *unsecured creditors*. Whatever is left over is distributed to the shareholders. Usually, that's nothing at all.

A corporation may never be discharged from bankruptcy. In a personal bankruptcy, the bankrupt person may be discharged four months to several years after the bankruptcy, depending on his or her conduct and the reasons for the bankruptcy. The court may discharge the bankrupt person absolutely, meaning that he or she is no longer responsible for his or her debts. Or it may require the person to honour part of the debts as a condition of being discharged. Certain obligations, such as alimony and maintenance, are not wiped out when someone is discharged from bankruptcy. Until discharged, a bankrupt person cannot be director of a company. His or her assets belong to the trustee, and he or she may be required to give a portion of the salary to the trustee.

PERSONAL ASSETS

In the case of a proprietorship, all personal assets of the owners go to pay creditors. With a limited company, the trustee can seize only company assets. In real life, the assets of shareholders in limited companies aren't usually protected fully. Revenue Canada will attempt to collect withholding tax from the directors if they can't recover them from their companies. If fraud or serious breach of duty are involved in the insolvency, principals will be held personally responsible and may face criminal prosecution. To obtain startup financing, businesses usually have to offer some kind of personal guarantee. The holder of the guarantee can seize the personal assets given as security if the business fails.

After secured and preferred creditors' claims have been settled, there's often nothing left for unsecured creditors. If they receive anything at all, it's usually a paltry few pennies per dollar of debt. After all, if the firm could pay its debts, there would be no reason for it to go bankrupt. For that reason, unsecured creditors may be open to proposals to reduce the debt.

RESTRUCTURING

For an insolvent business to work out of its problems, the first order of business is to look at its assets and liabilities, as well as security given to third parties such as banks, to see if there's any hope at all of a solution. You'll need the help of your professional advisers to determine whether a solution is feasible, and if so, to develop a proposal for your creditors.

FORMAL PROPOSALS

A firm may make a formal proposal to its creditors under the Bankruptcy Act. Together with a licensed trustee in bankruptcy, the firm develops the proposal. Trustee, creditors and representatives of the insolvent firm then meet, and creditors vote on the proposal. If it's accepted by a majority of creditors representing a majority of the total debt, the proposal is sent to the court for approval. Once approved, the proposal is binding on all unsecured creditors, whether or not they voted in favour of it. If it's not approved by either the creditors or the court, or if the debtor firm violates its terms after approval, the firm is placed in bankruptcy.

A proposal may simply involve getting more time to pay the debt. The firm may propose paying a portion of the debt over a specified period, for example 25 cents on the dollar over one year. If its future outlook is bright, it may offer a percentage of profits or shares in the company in exchange for discharging all or some of the debt. It may offer to sell specified assets and distribute the proceeds to creditors, keeping only the assets needed to run the business. Or it may simply ask for time to develop a solution. Under the act, the firm must offer the same terms to all unsecured creditors.

INFORMAL PROPOSALS

A firm may be able to develop an informal solution with its creditors. It approaches each creditor individually, outlining its debt-restructuring proposal. Creditors are not bound to accept it. Unlike formal proposals, the debtor firm is not automatically put into bankruptcy if the proposal is rejected. However, merely proposing debt restructuring may lead creditors to put the firm into involuntary bankruptcy. Thus, informal proposals are much less common than formal proposals.

For a solution to work, the problems that led to the crisis have to be addressed. If the problem is mismanagement, the firm may bring in a professional manager, or as Mulock did, take a crash course in the aspects of the business that led to the problem. If the problem is undercapitalization, the firm may bring in another investor. If the problem is a change in the market, the business has to adapt to the change.

Because of inexperience, new firms are more vulnerable to crisis than entrenched companies, notes Memorial University's Pynn. "New businesses learn by making small mistakes. If they don't make any big mistakes, they'll know their businesses inside out after a few years."

But as Mulock's and Cameron's experiences confirm, crisis can overtake established companies as well. Next to the startup phase, a business may be most vulnerable when it's going through a period of rapid growth: witness again the history of Tasty Chip Steak Products and Cameron Window & Glass. Growth throws a whole new set of marketing, management and financial challenges at owner/managers. We'll examine those challenges in the next chapter.

13/Managing Growth:
When Small Business Becomes Medium Business

In 1985, it became obvious to Boyd and Boyce Taylor they'd have to find new customers for their fish products. Their company, T&H Fisheries Ltd. of Cox's Cove, Newfoundland, was producing marinated herring for the European and American markets.

Marinated herring had long been a favourite among certain ethnic groups, particularly European immigrants. But not many of their children and grandchildren shared their relish for the strong-tasting product. In addition, health concerns were eroding the market for the heavily salted fish.

Moving into traditional white-meat fish such as cod and flounder was out of the question. There was simply too much competition. "There's no room to grow in that business," explains president Boyd Taylor. Instead, the company looked at underutilized ground-fish species, such as herring, caplin and mackerel; then looked for markets where they'd sell. Herring and herring roe are popular in Korea, Taiwan and especially Japan. And caplin, a small North Atlantic fish, is considered a delicacy in Japan, when it's full of roe. These species are also popular in some U.S. markets, and in the Soviet Union. The timing was fortuitous. Norwegian and Icelandic fish processors, who also serve these markets, were experiencing shortfalls in supply. As a result, prices on these fish products were increasing.

To seize these opportunities, the Taylors had to develop markets. In some cases, they worked through brokers. In others, they dealt directly with foreign food processors and distributors.

To exploit these new markets, they had to sell frozen rather than marinated fish. Between 1984 and 1989, T&H Fisheries invested $2 million in freezing and other processing equipment. In 1988 alone,

$1.3 million was spent. But the investments have paid dividends. Before the upgrade, annual sales ranged from $1 million to $2 million. Five years later, they range from $5 million to $6 million.

The Taylor brothers aren't resting on their laurels. They can't afford to. They see new market opportunities in the Caribbean, South America, Africa and the eastern bloc, all of which need cheap protein products. In the second five years of its redevelopment program, T&H could double its sales, says Taylor. They'll need to upgrade their equipment to penetrate these markets, and to stave off competition from low-cost South American producers and efficient Norwegian and Icelandic fisheries. Having upgraded his processing operation, Taylor would now like to upgrade the methods used to harvest the fish.

"We're selling a poor man's product," Taylor comments. "The secret of success is to have low overhead and produce efficiently. In Newfoundland, we have tremendous fish stock. With some product lines, people here are very primitive in the way they harvest and process it. The proper technology to harvest and process the stock costs a lot of money. But if we invest in good technology, this is our chance to grow."

THE GROWTH IMPERATIVE

The Taylor brothers had a simple choice: expand, modernize and find new markets, or watch their company slowly die. That's happened with other Newfoundland ground-fish processors who relied on traditional markets, Taylor says.

Their situation isn't that uncommon. Companies that rely on old formulas don't survive when conditions change. Companies that grow and adapt do. If you've developed a novel business idea, it's probably just a matter of time before you will face competition. Stagnant companies are less able to face competition than growing, dynamic ones.

SURVIVAL

For a study presented at the 1988 annual meeting of the National Association of Business Economists, Bruce Phillips of the U.S. Small Business Administration examined the survival rate of American companies started between 1976 and 1978. Firms that grow by adding new employees have a much greater survival rate than zero-growth firms, Phillips found. Firms that added one to four employees had a six-year survival rate of 66.3 percent; survival rate for zero-growth firms was 27.5 percent. Survival prospects for firms that grow early are greater than for those that grow late.

When a company enters a growth mode, it's almost as if it's back in a startup situation, says Catherine Swift, chief economist for the Canadian Federation of Independent Business. An existing company expanding into new products or new markets has to research its market, just like a new venture. It usually has to obtain financing to fund the growth, just as new companies have to obtain financing. "To take a leap, you need money and staff," comments Swift. "Neither is easy to come by."

THE COST OF NOT GROWING
Certainly for T&H, growth was imperative. Taylor says his company wouldn't have survived without the move into frozen fish. Some herring processors on the island have folded, he says. "We survived because we saw the danger signs. Others saw them too; but they couldn't put the financing together to move into frozen product."

To finance their expansion, the Taylor brothers had to do as much research as a new company. By showing how harvesting underutilized ground-fish species would extend the fishing season and increase employment, they were able to obtain grants and interest buydowns from the Atlantic Canada Opportunities Agency, a program operated by the federal Department of Industry, Science and Technology. The agency put up approximately $225,000.

The rest came from term and operating loans by the Taylors' bank. To obtain bank financing, they researched all their markets, demonstrating the probable return on their investment. Their predictions weren't rosy, pie-in-the-sky daydreams. They presented alternative scenarios, showing what would happen if, for example, the harvest was particularly poor in a given season. In the fishing industry, that's a very real possibility, Taylor notes. "Growth in this industry isn't steady or predictable. You might lose $100,000 one year and make $300,000 the next. But the numbers tend to average out."

GROWTH STRATEGIES

T&H Fisheries grew by expanding into new markets, and developing new products. Similarly, The Steals People, the office-equipment retailer we met in Chapter 5, has grown by opening new stores and by adding new product categories. However, that's not the only strategy open to companies that want to grow.

NEW PRODUCTS

A company can simply add new products to its existing line. Vancouver-based Vortek Industries Ltd., for example, sells high-powered lamps used in the aerospace and semi-conductor industries as heat sources for manufacturing processes. Vortek knew from its customers that there were markets for lower-cost lower-power lamps. "For some applications, our lamps are too expensive," explains president Gary Albach. "A lamp suitable for processing lower-temperature materials will open up new markets for us." He expects the new line to double his company's sales.

Scandinavian Record Import, the record distributor we met in Chapter 4, has grown by continually seeking out new product lines. It started in 1979 with a couple of obscure labels. Now it has over two dozen labels, some quite established. President Greg Pastic attends music-industry tradeshows around the world, looking for new labels.

NEW MARKETS

Alternatively, a firm can stick with the same products, but expand into new markets, perhaps by exporting to other countries, as T&H did; perhaps by opening additional stores. Magnum Dynalab, the stereo-equipment manufacturer we met in Chapter 1, has grown by developing export markets in the United States, Asia and Europe. Japan Camera Centre, the photographic retailer we met in Chapter 7, has expanded by opening new stores across Canada.

Finally, a company can grow by improving its performance with existing products and existing markets — by doing the same things it has always done, but doing them better. Whatever direction a firm grows in, it should be a logical extension of its current activities. Vortek's growth is based on its strengths: its experience in building light sources for manufacturing processes, and its reputation with its customers.

PLANNING

When existing businesses add new products or expand to new markets, they have to ask the same questions as do new businesses. Do customers want this new product? What will it cost to produce it? To market it? Can I make money on it? Are the customers in a new location my target customers? What are potential sales? What additional costs will I face in this location? Are potential sales enough to cover additional costs?

However, existing companies have some advantages. For one thing, they can use their customer base to determine a new product's likelihood of success. Vortek knew there was a market for lower-power lamps. The key question was whether the lamps could be produced at a price the market was willing to pay.

Soon after The Steals People opened, it held a contest. Anyone who deposited a business card in a drum became eligible to win a prize. By looking at the cards, management determined that most of the firm's customers came from small- and medium-sized businesses, and that many worked out of their home. That helped them fine-tune their store's product mix and service policies.

FROM STRENGTH TO STRENGTH

Next, the company looked more closely at its customer base. At that time, The Steals People concentrated almost entirely on computers and related products. But customers were asking about other business products as well: FAX machines, telephones, answering machines and photocopiers. As instructed, sales staff relayed these requests to management. The store added these products on a trial basis, and they sold extremely well. The Steals People has also added new products on suppliers' advice, again on a trial basis. "It works in both directions," explains president Howard Cracower.

When the firm opened its sixth store in mid-1989, it embarked on a new direction. In addition to business equipment, the new store in London, Ontario, offers business supplies: cheque writers, stationery, copy holders. In total, the company added 1,000 new items. The Steals People had already tried some of these in its other stores. "We'd put a display of pens or diskette labels by the cash register," Cracower explains. "You wouldn't normally find them in a computer store, but they took off." The reason was simple. These are items The Steals People's customers — small-business operators — use on a daily basis. Additional sales aren't the only advantage to the new products. "The more kinds of business products we can offer our customers, the more often they'll come in."

FINANCING STRATEGIES

It costs money to grow. Vortek needs to add another line to

manufacture its new lamps. For The Steals People to offer office supplies as well as computers and related products, it will need 12,000 to 15,000 square feet per store, rather than 7,000 to 8,000. And of course, it costs money to open new stores. Money has to be found for fixed assets, such as store fixtures, and for current assets such as inventory. Similarly, T&H Fisheries had to raise money for its freezing equipment. Even when no new capital assets are required for expansion, growth usually results in higher inventory levels and accounts receivable. Financing them can become a burden.

BANK FINANCING

As we've seen, T&H financed its expansion with bank loans plus some government grants and subsidies. To get the loans, the Taylors had to present a strong and thorough business plan, just as any new company would.

Bank financing isn't always possible, notes Swift of the CFIB. Often, businesses have exhausted their sources of debt financing to get the business up and running.The steepest part of a company's growth cycle usually occurs while the firm is still young. Thus, it may lack the track record a banker wants to see, she notes. To grow, a company may have to attract equity rather than assuming debt. Many entrepreneurs are reluctant to do that, Swift observes, because they're unwilling to forgo control of their companies.

EQUITY FINANCING

The Cracower brothers financed their growth by selling a minority share in their company to an investment company. The investor has an option to purchase 50 percent of the firm. With the additional capital, the Cracowers plan to open four to six stores a year over the next three years. For growth that rapid, a partner with deep pockets was absolutely essential. "When you become a $100 million company in five years," Cracower notes, "you don't do it on a shoestring."

As we saw in Chapter 1, Manfred Breunig had to bring in a partner to bring his new FM tuner to market. In 1985, he sold 51 percent of his company to Larry Zurowski for $400,000. That capital enabled Magnum Dynalab to grow from $250,000 to $800,000 in sales in one year. As Breunig observed, instead of 100 percent of a dead company, he now owns a minority share of a growing company.

INTERNAL FINANCING

Since then, Magnum Dynalab has financed growth from profits. "In our industry, we know it costs 35 cents on the dollar to finance increased inventory and receivables," Zurowski elaborates. "If we want to grow by $400,000, we have to come up with $140,000. It comes out of profits, so we don't cut prices. If we do, we won't be able to grow the way we want to."

FRANCHISING

Like Magnum Dynalab, Japan Camera Centre Ltd. has financed its growth internally. Between 1981 and 1989, the photographic chain we met in Chapter 7 grew from nine to 160 stores. It achieved this remarkable growth through selling franchised photo-finishing/camera retailing outlets.

But this strategy isn't for everyone. "More skill is needed in managing a franchise organization," Asa comments. "But you can get better results. Franchisees are more dedicated than most employees."

GROWTH CHALLENGES

Marketing and finance aren't the only challenges faced by growing companies. When a company expands, it may find it needs new management skills. As with a new company, a skills gap isn't critical as long as the firm is aware of it and does something to fill it. In Chapter 1, we saw various ways of adding skills. Manfred Brennig brought in partners with finance and marketing skills that perfectly complemented his technical and manufacturing skills. Owner/managers can also acquire the skills they need, hire people with the required skills or retain outside professionals.

The investors who bought into The Steals People helped the Cracowers fill their skills gap. "We needed expertise we didn't have – in finance, in real estate, in management of personnel and systems," Cracower remembers. "They have a group of senior executives who are experts in all those areas. Their services are available to us. We couldn't expand as quickly as we are without experience; and we couldn't afford to hire it." Concludes Cracower: "The average small business has a very difficult time making the jump to medium business. We saw it coming."

DELEGATING

While a company's small, the owner can usually manage every facet of the firm's operation. If an employee has a question or problem, he or she can usually get an immediate response from the boss. That can change when a company grows. The owner can't look after everything, so must establish a layer of middle management to act as a buffer. That can lead to all kinds of problems. First, many entrepreneurs find it difficult to delegate. Second, it can be hard to identify people with the right skills to act as management. A good sales person isn't necessarily a good sales manager.

Cracower addressed this problem by identifying his own skills and priorities. Where he can most help his company is in marketing, he concluded. He's determined not to lose touch with the sales floor. "Our aim is to be with our sales staff." He has hired and retained managers to look after administration, appointed regional managers to act as interfacers between upper management and retail staff. "We've been great at moving people up," Cracower says. "With 200 people in your organization, you can find a lot of talent." Cashiers have become sales people and administrative assistants. One person, hired for sales, has been promoted to store management, then regional management and finally purchasing. "We've learned how to delegate. The critical thing is to have senior people who can do your job as well as you can."

Culture

It's important to let senior people do their jobs. That means letting go a little. Inevitably, these people will change the feel of the firm. If they're talented, they'll superimpose their own personalities on the personality of the company.

Phillip Bliss's marketing services company began as a two-person partnership in 1985. Within three years, The Creative Marketing Network had a staff of 10. Net revenues grew from $600,000 in year one to $2.4 million in the company's third year. Then in late 1988, it merged with another firm, becoming G&S – The Creative Marketing Network, in the process growing to 45 people.

The growth has definitely changed company culture, says Bliss, vice-president of the merged firm. "There's a lot more going on, a lot more you can't control. You can establish reporting mechanisms; but you have to rely on others as much as yourself." In effect, these people become "partners," in terms of responsibility if not ownership. "That's all that counts in day-to-day operation," Bliss observes. "You're dealing with different personalities. Before I could just say, 'Do this.' Now I can't say that as forcefully. I need the approval of those who report to me at a senior level because I have to rely on them to implement decisions. I can't be there to do it. That's especially true in the creative business, more so than, say, in manufacturing."

UNPLANNED GROWTH

Growth-related problems are worse if the company isn't prepared for the financial and management challenges that come with growth. A sudden increase in sales can be a mixed blessing. As we've seen, increased receivables and inventory can be a real financial burden for companies unprepared for growth. Operating expenses can increase dramatically, to the point where the company isn't making money. That can prove disastrous if the company isn't getting regular and accurate financial information.

"Unplanned growth is one of the worst things that can happen to a business," comments Toronto businessman Gordon Hunter. "If the growth is based on an unknown quantity, the company can take on fixed overheads based on anticipated growth rather than reality. If you're growing 15 percent a year, you can plan. If your business is doubling every year, you can lose touch with reality. Everybody wants to lend you money. Everybody wants to work for you. You say yes to things you shouldn't. Then there's a correction, and the overheads don't go away."

HINDSIGHT

That's exactly what happened to Hunter. When the clients of his tradeshow and publishing company cut back promotional plans during the 1981-82 recession, Hunter developed tradeshows and publications for the computer vendors, some of whom were already clients. While the rest of the economy was in the doldrums, the computer industry was expanding rapidly. Hunter's business grew along with it. "We had very impressive growth," he recalls. "It looked like it would never end, until the computer industry hit a downturn." Companies big and small were shocked by the computer-industry shakeout of 1985.

"We misread the market," he reflects, with 20-20 hindsight. "There can be too much of a good thing." Hunter's wasn't the only company caught in the shakeout. Atari Inc. went from a $500 million profit one year to a $500 million loss the next. "That's a billion-dollar swing," says Hunter. "They thought Pac-Man would never end." In the end, Atari's owners sold the concern.

Hunter was able to downsize and retrench. "We weren't a casualty of our own growth, but we were a victim." He says he's wiser for the experience. If he were doing things over again, "I'd be more realistic and more cautious. I'd be a person who doubts. You have to plan for expansion. In terms of hiring and expenses, you have to look at your worst-case scenario. You have to staff for the slowest months. I'd rather pay for extra temporary help at peak times, than have staff twiddling their thumbs in slow times."

PLANNED GROWTH

Cracower's growth may be rapid, but it is planned. Even before he opened the first store in 1986, his plan was to build The Steals People into a 16- to 20-store chain with $100 million a year in sales. But he knew he couldn't do this overnight. For the first year, he operated just a single store, fine-tuning his concept and putting systems in place. "We wanted to take our time to make sure we understood what we were doing," Cracower explains. "By October 1988, we knew we were ready to take off."

We can see how Cracower proceeded. His company started with specific objectives — a 20-store, $100 million retail chain — and a timetable to achieve those objectives. The firm worked out a plan to achieve its goals: expansion into new locations and new product categories. When Cracower saw the potential of FAX machines and phone products with his customers, he grabbed the opportunity. Finally, he assembled the financial and management strength to put his plans into action.

Boyd and Boyce Taylor did much the same. Having identified a real threat to their current business — changing consumption patterns in their principal markets — they identified new markets and developed new products for them. After researching their market and the technology they'd need to address it, they were able to convince their bank that their expansion plans were viable. At the same time, other Newfoundland companies were failing because they lacked the marketing and financial expertise necessary to expand.

FOREVER ENTREPRENEURIAL

Starting your own company is a risky business. The risks don't stop once a firm's entrenched. Complacent firms can easily fall victim to changing market conditions or hungry competitors. Successful companies never stop taking risks, but move carefully to minimize them.

In 1959, John Asa and his brothers started with a single store on Edward St. in Toronto, just off Yonge St., the city's main shopping area. Then an opportunity arose to rent a store on Yonge St., but at four times the rent they were paying. They took the store, and sales increased four to five times. A few years later, they opened a store in a suburban Montreal mall on the advice of the developer's agent. At that time, the mall was just an empty field, but they knew the agent and trusted his judgment. He rewarded that spot by leasing them a store in a premier Toronto mall a couple of years later.

In 1962, the camera retailer had a chance to move into a related area when an opportunity arose to distribute Japanese Ricoh cameras. The brothers set up a second company, Ricoh of Canada Ltd., to sell Ricoh cameras and other photographic products to camera retailers, including Japan Camera.

Seizing the Opportunity

In 1978, Japan Camera seized the opportunity to enter a brand-new business when it obtained the exclusive North American distribution rights for a free-standing photo-finishing machine that could be located in stores. Company president Roy Asa saw the machines at a major industry tradeshow, and recognized the firm's president, Mr. Nishimoto, whom he had met before. The technology was brand-new at the time, but most people in the photographic industry dismissed it as a gimmick. The Asas, however, had faith in their own judgment and in Nishimoto's.

Today, the company that started as a single store off Toronto's main drag has over 160 stores and annual revenues of over $100 million. John Asa says there are several reasons for his company's success. One is humility: willingness to learn from other people's experience. Another is curiosity: willingness to search out and try new ideas. Finally, there's entrepreneurial drive: willingness to take risks and seize new opportunities.

There's a lesson here for all companies. Firms such as Japan Camera, The Steals People, T&H Fisheries, Magnum Dynalab, G&S – The Creative Marketing Network succeed because they maintain their entrepreneurial spirit. They keep on taking new risks, trying new ideas.

But they're not reckless in their risk-taking. They grow by design, not by accident. They plan their moves carefully, building on strengths they already possess. They also know their weaknesses; and take measures to counteract them. They make sure they have the financial and management resources to support their growth. They're disciplined. They know what business they're in, and they build on it, rather than going off on tangents. Finally, they're aware of things that made them successful, and they keep on doing them.

Index